Śuddha Bhakti

the path of pure devotion

Śuddha Bhakti

the path of pure devotion

Swami Bhakti Vallabha Tīrtha Mahārāja

MANDALA
publishing group

Singapore San Fransisco New York

Mandala Publishing Group

1585-A Folsom St.
San Francisco, CA 94103 USA
phone: 415 621 2336
fax: 415 626 1510
mandala@mandala.org
order online at www.mandala.org

ISBN: 1-886069-36-0

Printed and bound in India for Palace Press International

śuddha-bhakata-caraṇa-reṇu
bhajana-anukūla
bhakata-sevā parama-siddhi
prema-latikāra mūla

The dust from the lotus feet
of pure devotees is conducive
to devotional service,
and service to the Vaiṣṇavas
is itself the supreme perfection
and the root of the tender
creeper of divine love.

❧ Contents ❧

Preface

Śuddhā bhakti is a book about pure (*śuddhā*) devotion (*bhakti*). Such a book should be of great value on the threshold of the third millennium when the world is overburdened more than ever before with war, intolerance, hatred and atheism.

Bhakti-yoga is the spiritual practice by which the soul can reunite (*yoga*) in love (*bhakti*), with the Supreme Lord, for only divine love makes life worth living. This reunion should not however be misunderstood as the merging of the individual soul (*jīvātmā*) with the formless, all-pervading aspect of the Absolute, the Brahman. Love is a relational affair and *bhakti-yoga* implies an eternal relationship between creator and created, sustainer and sustained, lover and beloved, or God and the soul.

The immortal *Bhagavad-gītā*, probably the most celebrated and widely-read sacred text of ancient India, stresses the importance of *ācāryopāsana*, or adherence to the spiritual guide, for all those who wish to reconnect with the Divinity. Elevated and self-realized souls who can awaken one's spiritual nature are, as the *Gītā* states, very rare. We therefore feel fortunate to present this book of selected discourses by Śrīla Bhakti Vallabha Tīrtha Mahārāja, in whom we recognize all the characteristics of pure devotion. He is a humble but powerful practitioner and teacher of the Gauḍīya Vaiṣṇava tradition of divine love propagated by Śrī Chaitanya Mahāprabhu, the 15th-century master of devotional ecstasy. This book is compiled from lectures given on his second visit to Europe in 1999.

The first part of this book, entitled *Sambandha*, delineates the foundation of knowledge necessary to enter a life of devotion. Part two, entitled *Abhidheya*, discusses the means of practice, *sādhanā*, in which a *sādhaka* must engage to attain the desired result (*sādhya*). For the followers of Śri Chaitanya this goal is *prema-bhakti*: spontaneous, unalloyed loving devotion to Vrajendranandana Śrī Krishna, the divine Gopāla (cowherd boy) of the beautiful transcendental pasture grounds of Vṛndāvana, Whom the Gauḍīya Vaishnavas accept as God Himself. This ultimate aim is also known as *Prayojana*, the title and focus of the last chapter of this book.

We hope that all practitioners—aspiring, novice and advanced—will relish this book. We pray to Śrīla Tīrtha Mahārāja for his continuous blessings upon all sincere *sādhakas* pursuing the path of devotion. May Śrī Krishna be pleased with this attempt to serve the lotus feet of His pure devotee.

with humility,
the publishers.

Swami Bhakti Vallabha Tīrtha Mahārāja

Śrīla Bhakti Dayita Mādhava Mahārāja

Śrīla Prabhupād Bhaktisiddhānta Sarasvati Ṭhākur

Śrī Śrī Rādhā-Kṛṣṇa: The Divine Couple

Introduction

Three topics are discussed in the Vedas, the sacred scriptures of India. In Sanskrit, these are called *sambandha, abhidheya* and *prayojana*. *Sambandha* concerns the nature of ultimate reality: who is God, what is the essential nature of the soul and the world of our experience, and what is their mutual relationship? After obtaining knowledge of relationships, or *sambandha*, the practice of worship or devotion begins. This is called *abhidheya*, which is synonymous with *sādhanā* or spiritual practice. There are different kinds of *sādhanā*, but *sādhanā* proper is devotion or *bhakti*. What, then, is our ultimate goal—the *prayojana*? Our highest objective is love for Krishna, Krishna *prema*.

In the *Bhagavad-gītā*, Krishna states that He is the cause of all causes. In the ultimate sense, Krishna is considered to be the Supreme Lord because we can experience all varieties of relationships with Him.

Once we recognize Krishna as the supreme goal, how can we get love for Him, Krishna *prema*? The only way of getting Krishna is through *bhakti*. The *sādhanā* is *bhakti*, and the ultimate goal of our life and practices is *prema*—transcendental, divine love for Śrī Krishna. None of the four *puruṣārthas*, or aims of human life mentioned in the Vedas (*dharma*, *artha*, *kāma* and *mokṣa*) can be considered the ultimate goal. *Dharma* means mundane sacrifices performed for obtaining benefits in the upper worlds of the material universe. If we have a desire for *dharma*, we cannot attain the highest treasure of *prema*. *Artha* means wealth, *kāma* means fulfillment of lust, and *mokṣa* means desire for salvation. But none of these things will lead us to the ultimate goal of life, divine love of God. We have to perform *bhakti* to get Krishna *prema*. Our life is meant for the cultivation of *bhakti* and thus we should begin the process of devotion without a minute's delay.

Part One

Sambandha

The foundation of devotion

Sambandha

What is our conception of ultimate reality? Who is God? Who are the *jīva* souls, the living beings of the material world? What are the relationships between God, the soul and the world? In Sanskrit, knowledge of these things is called *sambandha* (relationship). These topics have been discussed in detail in the Vedas, the sacred scriptures of India, and all saints throughout history have spoken and expounded on their understanding of them.

Chaitanya Mahāprabhu preached the doctrine of divine love based on the evidence of the Vedas. Kavirāja Gosvāmī explained this in a nutshell:

veda-śāstra kahe sambandha abhidheya prayojana
kṛṣṇa prāpya sambandha bhakti prāptyera sādhana
abhidheya nāma bhakti prema prayojana
(*Chaitanya Caritāmṛta* 2.20.124-125)

What is the ultimate goal of life according to the Vedas? It is divine love for the Supreme Lord, Śrī Krishna. The etymological meaning of the name Krishna is "one who attracts and gives happiness to all." Krishna is the all-attracting principle. He possesses infinite qualities to attract us and is therefore the Supreme Person. He is the embodiment of all existence, all knowledge and all bliss.

There is nothing equal to Him or superior to Him. There cannot be more than one Absolute or more than one infinite being. If there is something outside the infinite, infinity loses its meaning and the infinite becomes finite. Not even a particle of dust can be imagined outside the infinite or outside the Absolute. The Absolute is defined as that which exists in, for, and by itself. Everything is within Krishna and everything is subservient to Him.

The infinite is one and it has a personal identity. God is the all-conscious substance. Consciousness implies three things: *jñāna*, *kriyā* and *icchā*—thinking, feeling and willing. When we look at the living beings of this world, we can see that a body is considered to be a person or a conscious unit for only as long as spirit is present in it. That which exhibits no thinking, feeling or willing is only matter and nobody considers dead matter to be a person.

The highest aspect of the absolute conscious substance is called Bhagavān and He possesses the three qualities of consciousness in an absolute way. If we can accept that an individual spirit soul is a person, then what is the difficulty in accepting that absolute consciousness is personal? He is an unlimited person. Though He has a distinct individual form, He is unlimited and exhibits innumerable forms and pastimes.

When a person takes the role of a king and sits on

his throne, he wears a certain kind of dress, but when he goes to the playground to amuse himself, he dresses differently. When he goes to bed, he will again change into a different kind of clothing. Throughout all these changes of dress, the person remains the same. The same principle applies to the Supreme Lord, who manifests different forms and pastimes for the sake of His loving devotees.

Even as a person, the Supreme Lord is infinite; His realms are infinite and an infinite number of souls emanate from Him. Human beings cannot fathom the Supreme Lord's creation by means of their finite intellect, finite mental capacity, and limited sense organs. He is beyond all our attempts to know Him by our own power.

Nothing cannot be the cause of something. All created things must have their cause in something other than themselves. We are like the particles of the sun that come from the sun, the substance. Just as the sun shines, so do its particles. Likewise, the Supreme Lord is the possessor of all kinds of potencies and the souls that emanate from Him are aspects of one of these potencies, just like the rays that come from the sun. The souls exist in Him, exist by Him, and they should exist for Him. But they can never be considered to be identical with the Lord, any more than the rays of the sun can be considered identical with the sun substance.

In seventh chapter of the *Bhagavad-gītā* ("The Song of the Lord") Krishna says with great emphasis,

mattaḥ paratarahṁ nānyat
kiñcid asti dhanañjaya
mayi sarvam idaṁ protaṁ
sūtre maṇi-gaṇā iva

"There is nothing superior to Me. The whole universe is emerging from Me. I am beyond the comprehension of the conditioned souls, the finite beings, and I am supremely superior to the formless *Brahman* and the indwelling *Paramātmā*, the objects of worship of the *jñānīs* and *yogīs*."

janma karma ca me divyam
evaṁ yo vetti tattvataḥ
tyaktvā dehaṁ punar janma
naiti mām eti so'rjuna.
(*Bhagavad-gītā* 4.9)

"My birth and My pastimes are transcendental. Unlike human beings who are compelled to take birth by their own previous actions, My birth is a pastime to satisfy My devotees. To give them parental service, I accept them as parents."

ajo 'pi sann avyayātmā
bhūtānām īśvaro 'pi san
prakṛtiṁ svām adhiṣṭhāya
sambhavāmy ātma-māyayā.
(*Bhagavad-gītā* 4.6)

"I have no birth, but I engage in these pastimes to fulfill the desire of those devotees who want to serve Me as their son. Those who are enveloped by My illusory energy consisting of the three primary material qualities, *sattva*, *rajas*, and *tamas*, think My body to be that of an ordinary human being."

We may think that Krishna is born in the way we were, but this is a mistake. As with everything else, Krishna's birth has both a morphological and an ontological aspect. Whatever we can know about an entity by means of our material senses and material intellect is its external or morphological aspect. But there is also an ontological side which we cannot know through our finite instruments.

Let us expand on this idea further. Immanuel Kant of Germany was one of western philosophy's most intelligent thinkers. In his critical philosophy, he named the above-mentioned aspects as "the thing as it appears" and "the thing in itself" or "the thing as it is." According to Kant, human beings can understand a thing as it appears, but have no capacity to know it as it is. In his *Critique of*

Pure Reason, Kant argued extensively to prove this contention.

Human beings, he says, can only know things as they appear to the senses and the understanding. Through the senses, human beings can perceive the forms of things and through understanding they can conceive of them in terms of categories. This understanding is a special capacity called *a priori*. Inherent in the capacity of human understanding is the ability to know a thing as it appears. But a human cannot have knowledge of the thing in itself. This is the basis of Kant's critical philosophy.

Another German philosopher, Hegel, tried to refute Kant's contention. According to Hegel, we may indeed arrive at knowledge of the thing in itself through speculative reasoning. Bradley, a British philosopher, also dealt with this problem in detail. His claim was that we cannot come into contact with the thing in itself by reasoning alone, but we can acquire knowledge of it through immediate perception and feeling, by which the thing in itself will appear before us. Otherwise, we cannot succeed in seeing things in their deeper quality through our capacity of reasoning alone. There will always be some barrier between the object of reason and the reasoning, and this prevents us from having contact with the thing in itself.

Now, these philosophers have tried to approach the ultimate reality with their intellectual arrogance. But what is the actual meaning of philosophy? *Philo-sofia*—love of knowledge. But what kind of knowledge do they pursue? They are only interested in empirical knowledge, that which is acquired by the sense organs, mind, and intelligence.

In the *Bhagavad-gītā*, the mind and intelligence are said to belong to the external potency of the Supreme Lord. According to the *Gītā*, that which is transcendental cannot be comprehended by the elements of matter, whether they be gross or subtle. But in this material world we are always trying to determine the ultimate reality through empirical processes.

In accordance with revealed scriptures like *Bhagavad-gītā*, the theistic aspect of Indian philosophy emphasizes the finite nature of human beings. Our intellect is finite; our mental capacity is finite, and anything produced by our mind and intellect must also be finite. Hence we cannot determine our ultimate cause because it is beyond the jurisdiction of these finite instruments. Anything a human being determines by his finite understanding will be a concoction. Therefore, we should not attempt to manufacture reality in our intellectual or mental factory. As conditioned souls, we are limited, as is our ability to gain knowledge through our own capacities. It is beyond the material intellect to determine the infinite.

The absolute truth exists always and it is our duty to find out how to see that reality through the deductive process. We cannot approach the absolute truth through the inductive process. So, how are we to see that truth? God is the cause of all causes; He is self-effulgent and self-luminous. We must therefore approach the truth of God through His grace.

When one is enlightened by the knowledge that destroys ignorance, all things are revealed in their absolute quality. The sun rises and lights up everything in the daytime. If you want to see the sun at night, is it possible? Even if you bring together all the lights of a great city like New York you will not meet with success. As the sun is self-luminous, your attempt to experience it will not work because your nature is intrinsically different from the sun's. You have to wait for the rays of the sun before you can see it. Your ability to see the sun will not decrease if you have no artificial light at all, any more than it will increase if you have an enormous searchlight. The light of this world cannot help us in seeing the sun. The sun's own rays alone can give us this capacity. Likewise, the Supreme Lord is self-effulgent, self-luminous, and by His grace alone will we be able to see Him.

In the *Bhagavad-gītā* Krishna has described two kinds of potencies: *parā* and *aparā*. The *parā* is the superior potency and the *aparā*, the inferior. One is spiritual, the other material. In the material world we find the eight elements that belong to the *aparā* potency: earth, water, fire, air, sky, mind, intelligence and perverted ego. The gross material body is composed of the five gross elements and the subtle body is composed of mind (*manas*), intelligence (*buddhi*) and perverted ego (*ahaṅkāra*), which is not the real ego. When we think of our ego in reference to the Supreme Lord, then we understand Him to be our master and that we, therefore, are His eternal servants. But when we focus on worldly things and think of ourselves as the enjoyers—then this is the perverted ego.

We feel some sort of pleasure or joy when engaged in sensual enjoyment, but the consequence is suffering. Disease inevitably follows unrestricted enjoyment. Ultimately, all acts performed on the basis of the perverted ego lead to suffering. So, the question is: shall we remain in this world eternally, perpetually causing ourselves such suffering?

The body has its origin, it will remain for some time and eventually it will perish. Whether the body you have received is very healthy or weak, it is not eternal. If you have good health and the capacity to enjoy, you will become so attached to your body as a result of your enjoyments that you will not want to leave it at the time of death. But still you will have to go. You will be taken forcibly by the messengers of death and your attachments will cause you much suffering.

Because they are enveloped in the illusory energy of the Lord, some people misunderstood this world; they think it is *ānanda*, or blissful, and that they can thus achieve happiness here. The Lord is the cause of this world. When people become averse to the Lord due to their relative independence, His shadow comes to envelop them. This shadow appears to them to be *sat-cit-ānanda*, eternally conscious and blissful, but in fact it has no actual substance.

Whatever you see is like a dream. While you are dreaming, you think you are seeing reality, but when you awaken from the dream you realize its falsity. In this sense, the whole world is a dream. When we awaken, we will see that everything in it is false, or *māyā*. *Māyā* means *mā-yā*, "not that." This world and the eight elements that comprise it are not eternal. However, the real self in contact with the world is something entirely different in substance.

apareyam itas tv anyāṁ
prakṛtiṁ viddhi me parām
jīva-bhūtāṁ mahā-bāho
yayedaṁ dhāryate jagat
(*Bhagavad-gītā* 7.5)

"There is another potency which is distinct from matter; it is known as the *parā* potency, the superior spiritual energy. The individual souls, the *jīvas*, are the outcome of the spiritual energy. They make up the marginal potency of the Supreme Lord Śrī Krishna."

In the *Gītā* Krishna says that the *jīvas* are His parts, but what kind of parts? Not parts of the substance, but parts of His marginal potency. Likewise, a particle of the sun's ray is not the substance of the sun.

This is the way we must understand the Supreme Lord's infinite potencies, or *śaktis*. We can divide these potencies into three main categories—internal, marginal and external—but in reality, they are infinite.

All souls are manifested by the marginal potency (*jīva-śakti*). When we become averse to Śrī Krishna, the external potency (*māyā-śakti*, or *aparā* potency) envelops us and we come to this world of birth, death and the threefold afflictions.

When we submit to Śrī Krishna, He will come in the form of grace incarnate or the internal potency. And the concrete form of the internal potency (*svarūpa-śakti*) is the *śuddha-bhakta*, the *sad-guru* or the spiritual guide. By the grace of the *śuddha-bhakta* we can enter into the transcendental realm of infinite bliss.

So what should we do and what should we not do? The main criterion has been mentioned in the *Padma Purāṇa*:

smartavyaḥ satataṁ viṣṇur
vismartavyo na jātucit

sarve vidhi-niṣedhāḥ syur
etayor eva kiṅkarāḥ
(*Bhaktirasāmṛta-sindhu* 1.2.8)

"You have to remember Krishna always. We have to do whatever is required in order to remember Him. For this reason the saints have prescribed many different forms of devotional practice. Outside of these principal devotional forms, other activities can be undertaken that will help us to remember Krishna. The criterion is that we should always remember Krishna and secondly that we should never forget Him."

Nobody on earth, whether atheist or theist, can prove that the body is the person. We consider the body to be a person only as long as consciousness is present in it. In fact, the existence that makes one a person, his real identity, is called *sat-cit-ānanda*. In the Sanskrit language we use the words *ātmā* or *jīvātmā*. You may use the word "soul" to identify the eternally existing principle within the body.

When consciousness leaves this body, the body no longer exhibits personality. You can preserve it chemically for a long time, but nobody finds happiness on seeing it. The life has gone. As long as the spirit soul, which is *sat-cit-ānanda*, is present in that body, it is considered a person.

Every living being has a profound desire to live in this world eternally. Eternal life, which in Sanskrit is called *sat*, is the demand of every sentient being. We all desire knowledge, which indicates that we have a knowledge principle, or *cit*, for something devoid of knowledge cannot have the desire to know. Similarly, if one is devoid of bliss, then one cannot desire bliss or *ānanda*. We all have the desire to get *ānanda*, we have the desire for knowledge, and we have the desire to exist eternally. These desires are the indications of our identity as the *ātmā* or *sat-cit-ānanda*.

Nobody wants to die, but we are enveloped by the illusory energy of the Supreme Lord that consists of three primeval qualities: *sattva*, *rajas*, and *tamas*. The material bodies of living beings are created by *rajo-guṇa*; once created, they are maintained and sustained by *sattva-guṇa*; ultimately, all are destroyed by *tamo-guṇa*.

When we are enveloped by this illusory energy, we get these temporary bodies. We take birth, we remain for some time, and then we die. We are not the non-eternal body but rather the eternal sentient being residing in the body, that is, the *ātmā* or soul. Krishna says in *Bhagavad-gītā*: (2.20)

na jāyate mriyate va kadācin
nāyaṁ bhūtvā bhavitā vā na bhūyaḥ

ajo nityaḥ śāśvato' yaṁ purāṇo
na hanyate hanyamāne śarīre

"This body is born, it will remain for sometime, and it will die. But the *ātmā* knows no birth and no death."

dehino 'smin yathā dehe
kaumāraṁ yauvanaṁ jarā
tathā dehāntara-prāptir
dhīras tatra na muhyati
(*Bhagavad-gītā* 2.13)

"After passing through childhood and youth, and after that, from old age to death, you will find that death is just another kind of transformation. When the body perishes, the *ātmā* will not perish. It is eternal. So we are eternal; nobody can kill us. We *are sat-cit-ānanda*, but we are running after *asat*, *acit* and *nirānanda*—that which is devoid of existence, devoid of knowledge, and devoid of bliss."

How can we get peace by cultivating these material things? What is the value of this eye? I could destroy it in a second with a stick and in a moment the whole world of vision would become completely inaccessible to me. I could also pierce my eardrum and the whole world of sound would be beyond reach. Such is the nature of the material senses.

How real is our experience if we depend on our

material senses alone? How real are our sensations? But if we recognize the indications of our real self, our *sat-cit-ānanda* nature, we live and feel the existence of the soul.

In one of the oldest holy scriptures of the world, the *Ṛg Veda*, it is written:

oṁ tad viṣṇoḥ paramaṁ padam sadā
paśyanti sūrayaḥ divīva cakṣur-ātatam
tad viprāso vipanyavo jāgāvāṁsaḥ
samindhate viṣṇor yat paramaṁ padam

"The lotus feet of the Supreme Lord are transcendental. He cannot be comprehended by the material senses, either subtle or gross. He is beyond the comprehension of mind and intellect. He is transcendental, *atīndriya*, beyond our sensual comprehension."

The Sanskrit word "*idam*" means "this" in English. When we experience with our material senses, we are seeing "this." But the lotus feet of the Supreme Lord are transcendental—"that." The object of devotion is one—the Supreme Lord's lotus feet. How do the devotees see Him? Is it through their own capacities? *Divīva cakṣur ātatam.* He is Self-effulgent; therefore, devotees who have His mercy can see Him. We cannot see Krishna without

His grace.

All the *jīvas* are eternally related to Krishna as parts of His potency. He is absolute. There is nothing greater than Him or equal to Him. Without His will, nobody has the capacity to know Him.

Some people give the following analogy to explain their understanding of the route to Krishna. They say: There is a great city called Rome. Is there only one road leading to Rome? No, there are hundreds and thousands of roads. Bhagavān, the Supreme Lord, is infinite. So to say that there is only one path leading to Him seems to be a dogmatic position. As He is infinite, there must be an infinite number of ways to get to Him.

However, this analogy is flawed. Rome is made of the five material elements of earth, water, fire, air and sky. It is nothing more than a lump of matter. In the same way, the gross body of the human being is composed of these five elements and the subtle body, of mind, intelligence and perverted ego is also material. But the real self, as stated above, is the outcome of the *parā* potency of the Supreme Lord Śrī Krishna. As long as the soul, the spiritual spark, resides in this world, it can dominate matter for it is superior to it. So a person can come to Rome in hundreds of ways because there is a spiritual spark inside the body. Even dogs can come, or ants because a spiritual spark is similarly present in those bodies. But Bhagavān, God, is not a lump of matter to be dominated. He is transcendental and we cannot dominate Him. We cannot get to Krishna without His grace.

In the scripture *Śrīmad Bhāgavatam* (1.2.11), it is mentioned:

vadanti tat tattva-vidas
tattvaṁ yaj jñānam advayam
brahmeti paramātmeti
bhagavān iti śabdyate

"*Tat* means 'it,' the transcendental, ultimate reality. This absolute, undivided knowledge is referred to by different words, *brahman*, *paramātmā*, or *bhagavān*. *Jñānīs* or knowledge seekers see the absolute in its *brahman* or all-pervading aspect of the absolute. *Yogīs* see it as *paramātmā*, the Supersoul present in every living being. And the devotees or *bhaktas* see it as *bhagavān*."

Bhagavān is the all-comprehensive idea. Bhagavān means one who possesses all kinds of opulences, namely wealth, power, fame, beauty, strength and renunciation. These are the six main opulences, but in reality they exist in infinite variety. You will not find an equivalent word for *bhagavān* in any other religion to describe the Lord in His fullness. Bhagavān is the greatest of the great, the smallest of the small, and everything in between.

Bhagavān takes many different forms, of which the sweetest is that of Vrajendranandana Krishna, the transcendental cowherd boy of Vraja. We can experience all varieties of bliss or *ānanda* by worshipping Śrī Krishna, but without His will nobody can see Him. We are not even able to see the president of a country without his permission, so what makes us think that we can see Bhagavān at our whim? It is faulty reasoning to think that we can see Him by any path of our choosing. If I can see a person by my own capacity, then he becomes the object of my experience and, in that way, subordinate to me. Likewise, if anybody sees me by his own capacity, I become subordinate to him.

Without the will of the Supreme Lord nobody can see Him, and to fulfill that will is called *bhakti*. If you want to serve somebody, what must you do? You have to satisfy him, and that means you have to act according to his will. Similarly, if we want to attain the Supreme Lord, we have to act according to His will. Why would God come to someone who has no desire to see Him? On the other hand, if God is compelled to come, He loses His position as God. *Karmīs* desire material benefit in this life and the next. They don't want Krishna, so why should He come to them? *Jñānīs* desire emancipation. They make no effort for the satisfaction of Krishna, so why should He come to them? We can only get Krishna through *bhakti*, exclusive devotion.

Everything is done by the will of the Supreme Lord. Without His will, nobody can do anything. If a person says that he can do something independent of the Supreme Lord's will, he diminishes the Supreme Lord's absolute position. Even a leaf cannot move without the Lord's approval. Furthermore, whatever is done by the will of the Supreme Lord is for the eternal benefit of all. He is all-good, omnipotent and omniscient.

Sometimes we think that what is happening to us is not just, but we do not really know how we are responsible for our own destiny. We do not know what we have done in the past and what reactions are now bearing fruit. Can anybody claim to have knowledge of their past activities? We even have difficulty recalling events from even two days earlier in our present life, what to speak of those from ten years ago. Can you remember everything you have done from morning to night? We forget everything. Such is our situation. We neither know what we have done in the past nor what will take place in the future.

When we do not see how to reconcile these things, we become worried, even unbalanced. But self-realized souls always reconcile themselves with even adverse circumstances. They are therefore always calm and serene. We, on the other hand, lack the proper vision and knowledge and cannot recognize the Lord's will.

Now one may ask, if even a leaf cannot move without the will of God, then it seems we do not have true free will. And what is the purpose of our lives if we have no free will? The answer is that living beings possess consciousness, which intrinsically means they have the power of thought, feeling and can exercise their will. But though the conscious unit has independence of thought, it is only a relative independence. There are many people who want to become a movie star or a president but are unable to fulfill their desire. One person who wants and needs to become president may attain his goal, but most will not. Our independence is thus relative.

Not all of our wishes come true. God controls all affairs, but He does not interfere in the relative independence of the *jīva*, the individual souls. He can interfere if He wishes, for He is omnipotent. But if He did so, then the individual consciousness would become inert; it would become matter. The independent consciousness would be destroyed. So the Lord Himself appears and tries to persuade the souls who are averse to Him to accept His teachings willingly. He does not want to force them to accept devotion. He could do so, but if He did, then the individual consciousness would be destroyed. What would be the benefit of that? Consciousness is a great wealth, so, while still maintaining the *jīvas*' relative independence, the Lord appears here in this world or He sends His own associates to make the *jīvas* understand that they should willingly submit to Him.

Once, there was a magician. A friend told him that

he was experiencing marital difficulties. He said, "I have everything I need, but my wife is not congenial. She is always doing something to displease me, so I am not happy. How can I control her? You are a magician. Can't you help me? You must know a spell or something." The magician gave him a magic wand and said, "Your wife will obey you, whatever you command."

The man went back to his house with the wand and ordered his wife, "Come here!" and his wife came. "Go there!" he said, and his wife went. "Sit here!" he commanded, and his wife sat down. But after doing this for some time, he realized he was still not happy. Why? Because his wife had become like a dog! He realized that for them to have a joyful relationship, she must have her independence, the ability to think independently. Only if she served willingly could there be happiness. If consciousness is destroyed, there can be no happiness. In the same way, God is not so ignorant that He chooses to suppress the relative independence of the *jīvas*. He retains it and His counterpart, Gurudeva, does the same. But they make the *jīvas* understand that they are the eternal servants of the Supreme Lord and that by serving Him they will become happy. They try to change the *jīvas*' mentality by showing them their own ideal character and example, and by explaining to and inspiring them.

God does not want to destroy the relative independence of His minute particles. With whom will He enjoy His pastimes? In order for service to exist, there must be both a servitor and a served. Only then does *prema* or divine love become a possibility. There can be no such love where there is only one person. The *jīvas* who are now here in this material world have forgotten Krishna, but ultimately, when they experience the awakening of the eternal nature of the self, they will cry for the Lord with great earnestness and perturbation. And God will taste and relish their emotion. Why should we deprive God of that pleasure?

My Guru Mahārāja once went to a place where there was a huge gathering. Everyone of all religions was welcome and so it was that half of the participants were Muslim and half were Hindus. One Muslim from the audience asked Mahārāja a question. "Swāmījī, have you seen the *ātmā* and *paramātmā*, the soul and the Supersoul? Can anybody say he has seen them? I think no one has ever seen the *ātmā* and *paramātmā* and that you are deceiving the world by speaking of them." Both the organizers of the meeting and the people in the audience were displeased with this challenger, but Guru Mahārāja answered him respectfully. He said, "You are obviously a learned person. May I ask you a question? What is the name of the book you are holding?" The man stated the name of the book. Guru Mahārāja replied, "I cannot see it. I cannot see the name of the book. You are deceiving me." Other Muslims came there and looked at the book's cover and confirmed the first man's statement. "Swāmījī, this man has told you the book's right name."

Again Guru Mahārāja continued: "I have my eyes and my eyesight is good. Yet I do not see what you say you do. You are collectively deceiving me. To me, it looks as though a crow stepped in ink and then walked on paper to make all those marks. I see nothing but crow's footprints."

Hearing this, the Muslim was enraged, "Swāmījī, do you not know Urdu?" "No, I do not."

The Muslim replied, "Then how can you expect to understand? You have to go through the alphabet and then you will be able to read it and understand. You have to earn the ability!"

Then Guru Mahārāja said, "You have given the answer to your own question. We have many kinds of knowledge. We may easily learn other languages, but we do not have the qualifications to know *ātmā* and *paramātmā*. We shall be able to see them when we acquire the necessary qualifications. Until we do so, we shall not be able to understand. I see the footprints of a crow, but other people see form and meaning in those footprints, because they have knowledge of the Urdu language behind their sight. If I have no knowledge of Urdu, I cannot see what you do. Once I have that knowledge I too will be able to see. In the same way, special eligibility is necessary to see the soul. You have to go to those who have realized this and ask them to help you understand."

When one is enlightened with the knowledge by which ignorance is destroyed, then that knowledge reveals everything just as the sun lights up everything in the daytime. This sort of knowledge is self-effulgent. You cannot see the sun at night because it is self-luminous; it cannot be seen with the help of other lights. When the sun rises and its light pours into your eyes, you can see the sun, you can see yourself, and you can see all the things of the world in their proper perspective.

In the same way when the self-luminous, self-effulgent Supreme Lord descends to a completely surrendered soul, then this soul will see his own self, he will see the other real selves of this world and all other things in their true perspective. All ignorance will be removed and everything will be illuminated by knowledge. But in order for this to happen, we will have to surrender to Him and take the help of the guru in every respect. We take the help of gurus, teachers, for even material knowledge, so why should it be different for the acquirement of spiritual knowledge? We have to go to a realized soul and take his instruction; then God will reveal Himself. We cannot know Him through our own ingenuity, nor with a challenging mood. God is an unchallengeable truth. He reveals Himself only to a completely surrendered soul.

The mind is the cause of bondage and the mind is also the cause of emancipation. This is stated by Kapila Bhagavān in the third canto of the sacred scripture, *Śrīmad Bhāgavatam*. Kapila Bhagavān was an incarnation of the Supreme Lord Himself who appeared as the son of Kardama Muni and Devahūti. One day Mother Devahūti asked her son, "How can a conditioned soul be rescued from the clutches of *māyā*, from all sorts of desires of this world? How can we rescue ourselves from the bondage of *māyā*?" To this Kapila Bhagavān replied:

cetaḥ khalv asya bandhāya
muktaye cātmano matam
guṇeṣu saktaṁ bandhāya
rataṁ vā puṁsi muktaye
(*Śrīmad Bhāgavatam* 3.25.15)

"This mind is certainly the cause of bondage, and this mind is also the cause of emancipation. How? *guṇeṣu saktaṁ bandhāya*. When the mind of a person is attached to *triguṇa*, the three primary qualities of the external potency of the Supreme Lord (*sattva-guṇa*, *rajo-guṇa* and *tamo-guṇa*), then he is in bondage. When the mind of a person is attached to *nirguṇa*, the transcendental Supreme Person, Śrī Hari, he will be delivered from the influence of *māyā* and will get salvation."

What is *triguṇa*? The living beings are created by *rajo-guṇa*. My body is created by *rajo-guṇa*, it is maintained by *sattva-guṇa*, and it perishes by *tamo-guṇa*. By *tamo-guṇa* the living being dies. Our body is thus *triguṇa*, because it is born, remains for some time, and then perishes. Our body is *triguṇa* in concrete form, so someone who always thinks about his body, its necessities and its beautification, is in bondage. Such a person only sees the tabernacle, the outside covering of the soul, and never the real self.

Take the example of a magnet and iron. What is the nature of a magnet? The nature of a magnet is to attract iron whenever it comes near to it. And the nature of iron is that whenever it comes near a magnet, it is attracted by it. But sometimes we see that both iron and a magnet are present, but the magnet does not seem to be attracting the iron, nor is the iron being attracted by the magnet. Why?

The Supreme Lord is attracting all. So His name is Krishna: one who attracts all and gives happiness to all. Krishna is supreme in all respects: He is the greatest of the greatest, *brahman*, the smallest of the smallest, *paramātmā*. He is the all-attractive principle. Still someone might say, "Swāmījī, you say Krishna attracts everyone, but He is not attracting me." But I say, yes, He is also attracting you, but you cannot feel it. Why? The magnet and iron are both there, but they do not attract each other because rust is covering the iron. Similarly, rust is now covering your soul and for that reason you are not feeling His attraction. You have to remove that rust or dust from your heart. If you remove it, your natural function will be awakened.

Due to your aversion to the Supreme Lord Śrī Krishna, you have been enveloped by His illusory energy and covered by the dirt of the world. You have to remove that dirt of ulterior desires. How can it be done? You have to remain in the company of *sādhus* or saints. You have to attentively hear with firm faith from a *śuddha-bhakta*, a pure devotee whose life is dedicated to Śrī Krishna and not from a professional speaker. There are many persons who say many things without acting on them. No speaker can bring about any effect in a listener without engaging in practical action, that is, without living according to his own teachings.

So you have to go to someone who is practicing, an awakened soul. Such a person can awaken many sleeping souls. If everyone is sleeping, who will arise? There must be someone to awaken others—an awakened soul. That awakened soul is the *śuddha-bhakta*. You have to hear from him attentively. The words that come from his mouth are a transcendental sound. You have to receive that sound through your ears and it will awaken the transcendental nature of your real self. That nature, love for Krishna, is present within you, but it is enveloped by the illusory energy and has to be awakened.

Does a diseased person possess the capacity to treat himself? When we are ill, we consult an expert, an eye specialist, ear specialist or heart specialist. We have to go to the doctor. The doctor may say, "Why have you come to me?" And we will answer, "Well, I do not have any knowledge of medicine. You can tell me what the cause of my disease is. Please examine me and tell me what is making me ill. Then prescribe medicine and the appropriate diet so that I may be cured."

If the doctor's diagnosis is correct and we follow his prescription of medication and diet, we will recover. As a diseased person I cannot treat myself. In the same way, all of us in this world are diseased, suffering from the threefold afflictions—miseries arising from our own bodies and minds, those caused by other living beings in this world, and those caused by natural calamities such as earthquakes. We are traveling through cycles of birth and death. You see that many babies are born—you were also born. You were once in your mother's womb like everyone else. And, like everyone else, one day you will also have to die. You have seen the types of affliction people are troubled by near the time of death—tremendous suffering—and your time of death is nearing.

As long as we live in this world, the threefold afflictions will exist. No happiness is permanent. The wheel of happiness and distress is always revolving. Sometimes you will enjoy material pleasures, then again you suffer. Suffering and pleasure follow each other regularly. When people desire for deliverance from these three-fold afflictions caused by the illusory energy of the Supreme Lord, they begin to inquire into their cause and search for a bona fide guru.

To take complete shelter of Krishna is called *śaraṇāgati*. It is related in the *Mahābhārata*, that when Duḥśāsana wanted to denude Draupadī in front of the kings and others such as Droṇa and Bhīma, Draupadī cried out Krishna's name, calling to Him to rescue her. Krishna did save her, but not immediately. Because He came to the rescue a little late, Draupadī complained to Him. She said, "Thank You very much for saving me, but You could surely have come a little earlier. Why did You wait so long? What is the reason You delayed?"

Krishna replied: "You called out My name, I admit. But those words were not enough. You did not take shelter of Me. At first you took shelter of Bhīma and Arjuna thinking that they would come and kill Duḥśāsana and protect you. Why should I come if you think that Bhīma and Arjuna can protect you? You uttered My name, but you did not take My shelter. You took shelter of Bhīma and Arjuna."

We cannot deceive Bhagavān. It is not possible. He is residing within us and sees everything.

Krishna: "Is it not true that you took shelter of Bhīma and Arjuna?"

Draupadi: "Yes."

Krishna: "Then why should I have come?"

Draupadi: "Well, You should have come after that."

Krishna: "After that you took shelter of Droṇa, the teacher of the Kaurāvas and Paṇḍāvas. If Droṇa had intervened, no one would have had the power to stop him. So why should I come if Droṇa could come and rescue you? Am I not correct?"

Draupadi: "Yes, You are correct."

Krishna: "After that you took shelter of grandfather Bhīṣma, the formidable warrior, and most respected member of all the court. If he had intervened, no one could have done anything... You took shelter of him. Why should I come if Bhīṣma could rescue you? You did not take shelter of Me. Actually, you were crying, 'Krishna, Krishna,' but you had not taken shelter of Me, but of those whom you could see before you. Why then should I have come? I thought, "Let them protect you."

"After that, you took shelter of Dhṛtarāṣṭra, and after that, all the other kings. After all that, you tried to rescue yourself by holding tightly onto your cloth—with one hand up you were trying to hold onto your cloth. But I do not appear where *śaraṇāgati* is only partial. I do not descend in such circumstances. When, you raised both your hands and called to Me, taking absolute shelter of Me, then I came immediately."

Unless we take absolute shelter, we cannot have any kind of remedy for our miseries. As long as we do not submit to the Supreme Lord Krishna sincerely, completely, we shall have to suffer the distress of this world. We are trying to earn money and maintain our worldly relations so that we might have happiness. Yet we can see the consequences of our attachment to non-eternal things—severe miseries. Even so, due to our ignorance, our misconception of self, we keep on trying for this ephemeral happiness. We have lost our money and we have lost our near and dear ones, but again we keep trying to get those things back again. If no human being is available, we acquire a dog, a cat, a parrot or whatever, and become attached to that. Again and again we try for the non-eternal because the root cause of our affliction is not eliminated. This root cause is our misconception of self and the ignorance of thinking that by getting material benefits we will be truly benefited. As long as we do not surrender to the Lord, we will never be able to attain the ultimate goal of life. The *Kaṭhopaniṣad* (2.23) mentions:

nāyam ātmā pravacanena labhyo
na medhayā na bahunā śrutena
yam evaiṣa vṛṇute tena labhyas
tasyaiṣa ātmā vivṛṇute tanuṁ svām

"God cannot be attained and realized by delivering lectures, by intellect, or by great erudition. The Supreme Lord will reveal His own eternal form only to a surrendered soul."

And at the end of the *Bhagavad-gītā* (18.65-66) Krishna has given His highest instruction to all conditioned souls of the world for their eternal welfare:

man-manā bhava mad-bhakto
mad-yājī māṁ namaskuru
mām evaiṣyasi satyaṁ te
pratijāne priyo 'si me

"Devote your mind to Me. If it is difficult to devote your mind to Me, serve Me; engage your senses in My service. If this is also not possible, worship Me. If even that is not possible, take absolute shelter of Me. I promise you that you will surely get Me."

sarva-dharmān parityajya
mām ekaṁ śaraṇaṁ vraja
ahaṁ tvāṁ sarva-pāpebhyo
mokṣayiṣyāmi mā śucaḥ

"Relinquish all My previous spiritual instructions about *dharma* (the relative social-religious duties enjoined by the Vedas) and take absolute shelter of Me."

The *Bhagavad-gītā* ends with *śaraṇāgati*, and that is where the *Śrīmad Bhāgavatam* begins. Without *śaraṇāgati* we cannot enter into the spiritual realm. So first we have to take shelter of Krishna. When one becomes a person who is of Krishna and does only things for the satisfaction of Krishna, then that is called *bhakti*. Hearing about His name, form, attributes and pastimes is completely transcendental. But first we have to take shelter of Śrī Krishna. We have to know that "I am of Krishna." That knowledge will be given by a realized soul, a *śuddha-bhakta*, or *sad-guru*. For that reason we have to go to a realized soul who is established in the eternal nature of the soul. He knows that he belongs to Krishna, and he is always serving Krishna. If we submissively approach such realized souls, inquire humbly from them and serve them, then they can awaken the nature of our eternal self. For that reason *śaraṇāgati* is necessary. And we can get actual *śaraṇāgati* by submitting to a *śaraṇāgata-bhakta*.

Śaraṇāgati has six aspects that are described as follows:

ānukūlasya saṅkalpaḥ prātikūlyasya varjanam
rakṣiṣyatīti viśvāso goptṛtve varaṇaṁ tathā
ātma-nikṣepa-kārpaṇye ṣaḍ-vidhā śaraṇāgatiḥ

"We should accept whatever is congenial for the service of Krishna. We should give up what is unfavorable. He is the only protector, and nobody else can protect me. And He is the only sustainer and maintainer. We should take absolute shelter of Him. We should be humble and give up our mundane material ego. These are the six divisions of *śaraṇāgati*."

Bhaktivinoda Ṭhākur ends his song about surrender, with the words, *rūpa sanātana-pade dante tāṛa kori, bhaktivinoda pore duhuṅ pada dhori.*: "With straw between my teeth I fall down at the feet of Śrī Śrī Rūpa and Sanātana." The point is that we have to go to a *śuddha bhakta*, a realized soul. He will impart knowledge of *śaraṇāgati* to us. If we do not submit to him, the process of surrender will never become manifest in us.

What then should we pray to Krishna for? We should pray to Krishna for the service of His lotus feet and that of His devotees. That is the highest prospect. "Please, kindly bless me so that I can get the association of Your true devotee. If I get the association of Your true devotee, I shall get You. Please give me this sort of blessing. Unless and until I get the dust of the lotus feet of a *śuddha bhakta*, I will never develop my love for Krishna." That should be our prayer.

PART TWO

Abhidheya

The practice of devotion

Abhidheya

Why should we try to get Krishna? Because if we can get the complete reality, we can get everything. By getting whom, we get all; by knowing whom, we know all—that is Krishna. We will have no want of anything else. All our desires will be fulfilled and all our problems solved. So how can we get Krishna? This is described by the *abhidheya* of *bhakti*, the practice of devotion.

One of Krishna's unlimited names is Hṛṣīkeśa. That means He is the enjoyer of all sense organs and their objects. Now if we do not engage our senses in the transcendental service of Śrī Krishna, then unholy things will enter our minds through those senses. That is why we have to stop them from engaging in material matters, so that mundane thoughts will not come into our minds. This can only be achieved by using our senses for the pleasure of the Lord under the guidance of a realized soul. Then, when Krishna is satisfied, He can give us the opportunity to see Him. That is called *bhakti*. This is the *abhidheya*, the method of spiritual practice as propagated by Chaitanya Mahāprabhu and substantiated by the Vedas. Only by loving another person can we increase our love for him or her. Similarly, if we want to increase our love for Krishna, we have to practice loving Him.

Those who say that Ultimate Reality has no form

and potencies are misguiding the whole world. He may not have a material form, but He does have one that is transcendental. If there is no form in the cause, then there can be no form in the effect either. God has infinite form and He can also take initiative. We can never find happiness independent of Him, but if we simply take shelter of Him, all our problems will be solved in a moment. What is the definition of *bhakti*? The following definition has been given in the scripture *Nārada Pañcarātra*:

sarvopādhi-vinirmuktaṁ
tat-paratvena nirmalam
hṛṣīkeṇa hṛṣīkeśa
sevanaṁ bhaktir ucyate

The word *upādhi* refers to the identities a person has acquired as a result of his previous actions. For example, if someone has a university degree, this will be the result of his own previous actions. Someone may think he has become an advocate, or a doctor, but these are external identifications. The real self is something different. Because of our previous actions we were born in different castes and different countries. But our castes and nationalities are all *upādhis*. If we engage in further actions on the basis of this ego, it will be *karma*, material activities for which we will get an opposite reaction, and not *bhakti*.

What is *karma* and what is *bhakti*? It is very difficult to differentiate one from the other. Simply stated, whenever we do anything with a sense of material ego, the results go to the material ego. When we take the merits of our actions for our own self, it is called *karma*—it is not *bhakti*. The results of all our actions should go to the Supreme Lord, not to our own pocket. Someone may work throughout the day and night inciting an observer to say, "This person is a very good servitor." But if he is doing this work to satisfy his own material ego, then it is not *bhakti*. For it is said, "*sarvopādhi-vinirmuktaṁ*." We should be completely free from all kinds of material identification. *Vinirmuktaṁ* means there should not be even a scent of material ego. If there is even a touch of material ego, there is no question of *bhakti*—it will be *karma*.

"I am from India, I am of such and such caste"—these are examples of material ego. There is no goodness in this world; all is *amaṅgala*, unholy. We become unholy when we think we are of this world. Anything done with the unholy ego is unholy. So we should have no connection with this world by completely freeing ourselves of this ego. This condition is very difficult to achieve.

However, just to be free from ego is not enough. *Jñānīs*, or knowledge-seekers also want to give up the ego. They want emancipation; they want to merge themselves with *brahman*, the impersonal formless aspect of God. But we cannot perform *bhakti* just by divesting ourselves of the worldly material ego. "*Tat-paratvena nirmalam:*" We should give ourselves to Him. We have to sincerely feel that we belong to Krishna and the guru in our hearts, not just mouth the words. Then we shall become sanctified, *nirmalam*. This is confirmed by another definition of *bhakti* that is given in *Bhakti-rasāmṛta-sindhu* (1.1.11):

anyābhilāṣitā-śūnyaṁ
jñāna-karmādy-anāvṛtam
ānukūlyena kṛṣṇānu-
śīlanaṁ bhaktir uttamā

"This is the best devotion, or *uttamā bhakti*: One should be free of non-devotional desires of any kind. All kinds of sin should be removed from the heart. We should not be entangled with *jñāna* and *karma*, knowledge aimed at liberation and reward-seeking activity. This is not helpful for getting pure devotion. And we should submit to a true devotee. *ānakūlyena kṛṣṇānuśīlanaṁ*—we have to act only for the satisfaction of Krishna."

This is the general meaning of the verse, but its real significance is to point us in the direction of Rādhārāṇī, the most perfect form of Krishna's potency. She is the highest devotee, and we have to take shelter of Her and Her extensions, the *sakhīs* and *mañjārīs* (girlfriends and maidservants). When, like them, we have given ourselves completely to

Krishna, then whatever we do after that will be devotion.

The different devotional practices, or *sādhanās*, have been explained in *Śrīmad Bhāgavatam*. Now there are two general kinds of *sādhanā* according to which we can practice *bhakti*: *vaidhī bhakti* and *rāgānugā bhakti*. *Vidhi* means rule or regulation. For those who have no natural love for Śrī Krishna, *vaidhī bhakti* is appropriate. There are many conditioned souls who have no taste for worshiping Krishna, because they have no feeling of relationship with Him. When one has a relationship with somebody, there is an automatic impetus to serve or love that person. Parents do not need to be taught to love their children. The tendency is there due to their natural relationship. However, very few of us have any feeling of relation with the Supreme Lord, so there are *vidhis*, rules and regulations. We are told : "He is the Supreme Lord. He is the Creator and Sustainer. It is our duty to worship Him." Most of us have no spontaneous liking for worship, but will practice devotion because it is the injunction of the scriptures. Thus for ordinary aspirants, *vaidhī bhakti* is applicable.

Rāgānugā means spontaneous attraction. Those devotees whose attraction to Krishna is inborn are called *ragātmikā-bhaktas*. They are the original associates of Lord

Krishna. No conditioned soul can become *ragātmikā*. But as conditioned souls we can have a relation with *rāgānugā bhakti*. *Rāgānugā-bhaktas* also have spontaneous love for Krishna, but they have developed it through *sādhanā*. If we can associate with them, then we might automatically develop a spontaneous love for Krishna that is very intense. But such cases are exceptional.

At present we worship the deities of Rādhā and Krishna on the altar according to many rules and regulations, our love being restricted by the injunctions of the scriptures. In fact, however, Rādhā and Krishna are the only possible objects of spontaneous love. The Vrajavāsīs, the inhabitants of Krishna's transcendental realm Vṛndāvana, think that Krishna is subservient to them. And the highest form of spontaneous devotion is found in Krishna's absolute counterpart, Śrīmatī Rādhārāṇī and her personal associates, the *gopīs*. If we take the *mantra* from the subordinates of Rādhārānī, the *sakhīs* and *mañjarīs*—then this *mantra* will take us to Rādhā and Krishna in their mood of service. At present, however, we have just started *sādhanā* and will not have this realization. We are thus eligible to perform *vaidhī bhakti*, but ultimately, if we go on practicing, then the desire to serve Rādhā and Krishna intimately will rise up automatically from the core of our heart. The *rāgānugā-bhaktas* also follow the *aṅgas* or limbs of *vaidhī bhakti*, but with intense love. If we practice sincerely, eventually such intense desire to serve will spontaneously arise from within. We have to be patient, and for now we have to continue practicing according to the guidelines of *vaidhī bhakti*.

Vaidhī bhakti consists of sixty-four principal limbs of devotion. Of these, nine are specified as essential in *Śrīmad Bhāgavatam* (7.5.23-24):

śravaṇaṁ kīrtanaṁ viṣṇoḥ
smaraṇaṁ pāda-sevanam
arcanaṁ vandanaṁ dāsyaṁ
sakhyam ātma-nivedanam

We have to hear about Krishna. And, after hearing, we have to chant about Krishna. We have to know about His transcendental name, form, qualities and pastimes. After we know about these we can speak about them. But first we have to go to those who have received this knowledge through the preceptorial channel. By listening to them, those transcendental sounds will come through our ears and touch and awaken our real self. That is the only way. We have to hear, *śravaṇa*, from an awakened soul and not from a professional platform speaker. After hearing we have to chant, *kīrtana*. And there are other forms of *sādhanā*, like *smaraṇa*, or remembrance. A devotee engages all his senses in the service of Śrī Krishna.

śravaṇādi-kriyā tāra svarūpa-lakṣaṇa
taṭastha-lakṣaṇe upajāya prema-dhana
(*Chaitanya Caritāmṛta*, *Madhya*, 22.107)

Svarūpa-lakṣaṇa means the original characteristic of a *śuddha-bhakta*. A pure devotee will always speak about Krishna and always hear about Krishna. As fish and other aquatic animals cannot survive without water, *śuddha-bhaktas* cannot survive without speaking about Krishna, hearing about Krishna. That is their life. When we engage in *śravaṇaṁ* and *kīrtanaṁ* with a *śuddha-bhakta*, the concomitant result will be love for Krishna. This love is innate in the nature of every living being. We cannot awaken it through penance and austerities, but this eternal nature of the self will automatically be awakened if we keep the association of *śuddha-bhaktas*.

Chaitanya Mahāprabhu in turn selected five principal forms of devotion: *bhāgavata-śravaṇa*, *mathurā-vāsa*, *śrī-mūrti-sevana*, *sādhu-saṅga*, and *nāma-kīrtana*. We should listen (*śravaṇa*) to the transcendental narrations about the Lord as found in *Śrīmad Bhāgavatam*. We should hear these narrations from *śuddha bhaktas* and in that way have association with them, *sādhu-saṅga*. And we should stay (*vāsa*) in a holy place like Mathurā or Vṛndāvana where Krishna performed His earthly pastimes. We have to stay in the transcendental realm. A place where devotees sing the glories of the Supreme Lord is also considered as a transcendental realm. And we should worship (*sevana*) Śrī Krishna in His Form as a *mūrti* (deity) on the altar with firm faith. Among these principal forms of devotion, however the foremost emphasis is given to *nāma-kīrtana*. Chanting the holy names of Krishna without offenses quickly removes all afflictions and bestows the ultimate goal of life, Krishna *prema*. We will now discuss these five principal forms of devotion in more detail.

Chaitanya Mahāprabhu propagated Divine Love based on the teachings of the Vedas and *Śrīmad Bhāgavatam*. Chaitanya Mahāprabhu was an erudite scholar. According to Śrī Chaitanya, the *Śrīmad Bhāgavatam* is the quintessence of all scriptures. Vyāsadeva, the compiler of the Vedas, stated in the *Garuḍa Purāṇa* that the significance of the Vedas has been retained and enhanced in *Śrīmad Bhāgavatam*.

How can we know about Krishna? We can only know about Him through the ears and not through the eyes. We can hear about the real form of Krishna from the *sādhus*, but unfortunately we think we have no time for hearing about the Lord. The noble king Parīkṣit Mahārāja heard from the sage Śukadeva Gosvāmī continuously for seven days without taking any food, without sleeping, going to bed, or even drinking water. Then he was able to attain the ultimate goal of life. But if we have no time to hear, how can we acquire knowledge about the ultimate goal? Even if you want to get material knowledge, you have to go to the appropriate teachers and hear from them. Likewise, there is no way to gain transcendental knowledge other than the ear. Of all our senses, it is the nearest to the soul.

It is said in the scriptures that *bhakti* can be achieved by the association of a bona fide *śuddha-bhakta*, a pure devotee. And who will get the association of a *śuddha-bhakta*? Those who have knowingly or unknowingly served Śrī Krishna accumulate a number of impressions in their psyche. These impressions develop into *śraddhā*, faith, and this faith in turn creates the impetus to go to a *śuddha-bhakta* to hear about the Supreme Lord. These previous impressions, which we call *sukṛti*, are the original cause of devotion. They are eternal and not material good deeds.

Now a *śuddha-bhakta* cannot have material desires. But for argument's sake, if any *śuddha-bhakta* wants and tries to get any of the temporary things of this world, God will put some obstacle in his way. If by mistake or ignorance a pure devotee desires to attain the heavenly planets or any of the things connected to the material realm, God will put obstacles in his path. Does this mean that God is not gracious to such a devotee? No, that is His compassion, His kindness, because He knows that the wealth of this world is poison to His devotee. The devotee has no real need for it. If we want to enjoy, we must come into contact with the temporary things of this world. But we cannot enjoy the Supreme Lord; we cannot enjoy the guru, or Bhagavān. We can only enjoy non-eternal things. When God sees His devotee is going to pursue non-eternal things, seeking the poisonous wealth of this world with the spirit of enjoying, He will not allow him to do so. Only those who have no ulterior motives can understand this. They can understand the compassion of the *śuddha-bhakta*, the pure devotee, and Supreme Lord. But those who have got ulterior motives think that they have been blessed when the Supreme Lord or Gurudeva fulfills their base desires. Only those who have no other desire can understand the actual mercy of Bhagavān.

Chaitanya Mahāprabhu has taught us in His *Śikṣāṣṭakam:*

na dhanaṁ na janaṁ na sundarīṁ
kavitāṁ vā jagadīśa kāmaye
mama janmani janmanīśvare
bhavatād bhaktir ahaitukī tvayi

"I do not want wealth. I do not want followers or salvation, and I don't want material knowledge. Please give me exclusive devotion to Your lotus feet. I want nothing else." If we want anything else besides this, repentance will automatically follow. When we get the association of the *sādhus*, real *sādhus*, we will be rescued from this world, its births and deaths and its threefold afflictions. Krishna sends His own person to rescue us.

When we are attached to Śrī Krishna, we will be emancipated, delivered from *māyā*. But Krishna does not talk to us; His *murti* stands silently on the altar. Out of many, many devotees, He might have spoken to somebody, but He does not speak to me. On the other hand, I know my body is perishable. I also know that other bodies are perishable, transitory, that they will not remain. Even so, in spite of knowing that they are temporary, I can exchange thoughts with them. Because we can speak and exchange thoughts with the living beings of this world, we become attached to them and our relations with them. But Krishna is only standing there silently, so how can we get attachment for Him? This is our problem.

Kapila Bhagavān shows us the solution. The *mūrti* of the Supreme Lord may not be speaking to you, but you can see the *śuddha-bhaktas*, the *sādhus* (saints); you can speak to them and exchange thoughts with them.

prasaṅgam ajaraṁ pāśam
ātmanaḥ kavayo viduḥ

sa eva sādhuṣu kṛto
mokṣa-dvāram apāvṛtam
(*Śrīmad Bhāgavatam* 3.25.20)

If you have the association of a *śuddha-bhakta*, a pure devotee, then you will be rescued. The *śuddha-bhakta* is always moving in this world.

Now there are six ways of associating with *sādhus*. This has been stated by Rūpa Gosvāmī in his *Upadeśāmṛta*:

dadāti pratigṛhṇāti
guhyam ākhyāti pṛcchati
bhuṅkte bhojāyate caiva
ṣaḍ-vidhaṁ prīti-lakṣaṇam

When we love somebody, what do we do? We give something that is dear to us and we accept that which is offered to us in return. It is give and take. We open our hearts to that person, and we listen to his heartfelt words. We serve him, feeding him with varieties of good food, and we accept the same in return. This is the way we associate with people in friendship. Now if we relate in this way with people who are in bondage, we will become attached to worldly things. But if we engage in such exchanges with *sādhus* it will lead to love for Krishna. If we give the *sādhu* something of this world, he accepts it and then engages it in the service of Śrī Krishna. Then, after sanctifying it in this way, he gives it back to us as *prasāda*, divine remnants.

I was told by my spiritual master that if you use donations given for another purpose for yourself, you are taking poison. You should give everything to guru and Vaiṣṇava and that poison will be destroyed by them. They have this power because they have been reinstated in their real selves. We do not know that everything belongs to Krishna, but they do.

Chaitanya Mahāprabhu directed Tapan Miśra to give Sanātana Gosvāmī a cloth. Sanātana Gosvāmī told the Lord that he would not accept a new cloth, but wanted one that had previously been worn by a devotee so that it would be *prasāda*.

Next we should open our hearts to the devotee—"*guhyam ākhyāti pṛcchati*." If we do not open our hearts, then the *sādhu* will not open his either; he will not speak about the esoteric aspects of *bhajana* or spiritual practice. He will only speak openly when he has examined a person and found him to be fit. We should therefore not be afraid to speak openly of our frailties. In this way, we will develop a heart-to-heart relation with the *sādhu*.

Next, we should feed the *sādhu* with great devotion and love. The *śuddha-bhakta* sees that Krishna is the only enjoyer and that all things belong to Him, and so he offers them to the service of Krishna, and after making the offering he will give you *prasāda*. If you take the *prasāda* with the knowledge that you are taking Śrī Krishna's remnants, you will be rescued from the clutches of *māyā*.

This is the way that we should associate with *sādhus*. If we engage in such exchanges with the conditioned souls, the sleeping *jīvas* of the world, we will become attached to them. So it is far more beneficial to cultivate such relations with a *sādhu*. But simply remaining near the body of a *sādhu* is not associating with him. Bugs and mosquitoes may come into close contact with the *sādhu*, but what are they doing? They are sucking his blood. To exploit the *sādhu* in such a way is not associating with him. You have to follow the mentality of the *sādhu*, the thoughts of the *sādhu*. The *sādhu* thinks about the service of Krishna and, if we follow that, then we can associate with him even when we are a thousand miles away. On the other hand, without that consciousness, we may be physically very close to him, even sleep in the same bed, but never gain any *sādhu-saṅga*. The *sādhu* is for the service of Rādhā-Krishna; we have to follow this idea of his. Actual association means remaining in contact with the *sādhu* in a serving mood.

Then Mother Devahūti asked, "You have advised us to associate with the *sādhu*. But who is *sādhu*? Please describe the qualities by which we can recognize a *sādhu*." Kapila Bhagavān replied that *sādhus* have two kinds of qualities: the *svarūpa-lakṣaṇa* and *taṭastha-lakṣaṇa*. *Svarūpa* means original or actual; so the *svarūpa-lakṣaṇa* refers to the quality without which no person can become a real *sādhu*. The real sign of the *sādhu* is that he does everything only for the satisfaction of the Lord. When this characteristic of the devotee is present, then the other qualities, the *taṭastha-lakṣaṇa*, will follow. What are these secondary characteristics? Kapila says:

titikṣavaḥ kāruṇikāḥ
suhṛdaḥ sarva-dehinām
ajāta-śatravaḥ śāntāḥ
sādhavaḥ sādhu-bhūṣaṇāḥ
(*Śrīmad Bhāgavatam* 3.25.21)

Titikṣavaḥ. A *sādhu* will be tolerant and forgiving. Why? They have no desire except the service of Śrī Krishna. If you have any other desire besides this service you cannot be tolerant. This is the meaning of the third verse of Chaitanya Mahāprabhu's *Śikṣāṣṭakam*:

tṛṇād api sunīcena
taror api sahiṣṇunā
amāninā mānadena
kīrtanīyaḥ sadā hariḥ

"We should be more humble than a blade of grass, more

tolerant than a tree; we should give respect to all and not want any respect from others."

This is the general meaning of this verse. Bhaktisiddhānta Sarasvatī Gosvāmī Ṭhākura pointed out that those who have a misconception of self can never become more humble than a blade of grass; they can never do *Hari-kīrtana* and perform *bhakti-yoga*. One who has a misconception of self will have bodily desires. He will have the desire for *kaṇaka, kāminī* and *pratiṣṭhā*—the desire for wealth, the attraction for sex, and the greed for respect, name and fame. When an obstacle to fulfilling his desires arises, he will be enraged. He will become unbalanced and intolerant. Outwardly he may show respect and tolerance, but it will be hypocritical. To become a *sādhu* is not so easy. A person with these qualities is rarely to be found.

Kāruṇikāḥ. The *sādhus* will be gracious, they will have compassion for all the *jīvas* of this world. The *sādhu* sees Krishna and that all is connected with Krishna, so he naturally loves all living beings of the world equally. According to their qualifications, *sādhus* may understand the behavior of guru and Vaiṣṇava in somewhat different ways, but their love is equal for all. They know the root cause of our affliction is forgetfulness of our relation with the Supreme Lord Śrī Krishna.

We are always sleeping—the nature of the body is that it is sleeping—but we should fight against this lethargy, otherwise we cannot worship Krishna properly. We may sleep all day and all night, but still we are drowsy. Look at the way the Gosvāmīs performed *bhajana*. They knew that we may leave this body at any moment and so they asked themselves, "Why should we spoil our time?" Worship of Krishna means to hear about Krishna. Hearing about Krishna is *bhakti*, speaking about Krishna is *bhakti*. This is our life. We should not spoil our time but should hear such things repeatedly.

Sometimes we say, "Oh I have already heard all these things." In fact we have not really heard. Chaitanya Mahāprabhu had heard the story of Prahlāda Mahārāja a hundred times and still requested His associates to speak about him. Such accounts are not composed of material sound; they cannot become stale. You can have the taste of spiritual ambrosia at every moment by listening to them. So we have to give up all our nescience and start Krishna *bhajana* without a moment's delay.

karau harer mandira-mārjanādiṣu
śrutiṁ cakārācyuta-sat-kathodaye
(*Śrīmad Bhāgavatam*, 9.4.18)

A devotee engages his ears in hearing about the glories of Krishna from a *śuddha-bhakta*. A *śuddha-bhakta* who has dedicated his life for the service of Śrī Krishna can speak about the glories of Śrī Krishna. This is *sat-kathā*.

Those who are platform speakers have some other motive. When they speak about Krishna, their aim is to get some money, name and fame, and so on. That is not *Hari-kathā*. *Hari-kathā* can only be spoken by a bonafide *sādhu*.

mukunda-liṅgālaya darśane dṛśau
tad-bhṛtya-gātra-sparśe 'ṅga-saṅgamam
ghrāṇaṁ ca tat-pāda-saroja-saurabhe
śrīmat-tulasyā rasanāṁ tad-arpite
(*Śrīmad Bhāgavatam*, 9.4.19)

"*Mukunda-liṅgālaya darśane dṛśau*. The *sādhu* engages his eyes in seeing the temple where the deities are worshiped and for the *darśana* of the deity. He engages his body in touching the Lord's deity form so that transcendental devotion may enter into him. If he finds a nice fragrant flower, he does not smell it but first offers it to the Supreme Lord, and afterwards he takes it as *prasāda*. *Pādau hareḥ kṣetra-padānusarpaṇe*. The *sādhu* engages his feet and legs for the service of Śrī Krishna by circumambulating the transcendental realm of the Supreme Lord and for bringing the articles for *pūjā*. In this way we should engage all our senses in the service of Śrī Krishna."

We can understand according to our individual capacity. A *śuddha-bhakta* sees Krishna directly; he speaks with Krishna. Krishna also moves with him, but not with us because we have got some sort of connection with this body, and bodily attachment is there. We cannot see because our eyes are not pure. We need *prema-netra*, devotional eyes that have been soothed with divine love. We can only see Krishna with devotional eyes.

It is not so easy to have *darśana* of Krishna for we can only see with spiritual, devotional eyes. We have the enjoying spirit; we are filled with lust. When the enjoying spirit pushes us to satisfy our senses, we come into contact with finite things, matter. We have thus suffered in death's prison for millions of years. This is our inheritance. However, when the eyes are for Krishna only, then Krishna will appear. So the *śuddha-bhaktas*, *uttama-bhaktas*, the best devotees, see Krishna everywhere. And they only take *prasāda*. They do not take what cannot be offered to Krishna. They always think about Krishna; pure devotees of the Lord have a liking for only remembrance and *kīrtana*. Day and night, they will hear about Śrī Krishna's transcendental name, form, attributes and pastimes from the lotus mouths of the devotees.

We should not see others' defects. If we want to rectify things, we should first see to our own defects. A real Vaiṣṇava or devotee is like a swan, a *haṁsa*. The *haṁsa* has the capacity to take the milk out from a mixture of milk and water. Vaiṣṇavas are *paramahaṁsas*. They see the good qualities in others and not the bad. All the sleeping conditioned *jīvas* have both good and bad qualities. Only realized souls have no bad qualities. Even so, they see the good qualities of others and ignore the bad. We, the conditioned *jīvas*, see the bad qualities and ignore the good. This is one reason we are in bondage. We need some rectification if we are to awaken from our state of bondage. The guru and Vaiṣṇava who have love for their disciples may sometimes correct them for their own good. They may control or chastise them, but that sort of chastisement or speaking of harsh words to the novice is not a reaction to the obstruction of their own ego desires or *kāma*. The *śuddha-bhaktas* have no *kāma*, so if perchance they should punish, they do so out of love.

Some people direct their anger or *krodha* to the *sādhu*, but we should not do this. To vilify a *sādhu* is a big offense and very detrimental to our spiritual welfare. To stop such offenses, pure devotees may express anger, but this for the spiritual benefit of the person who is committing the offense and not for some personal egoistic purpose. Not everyone is entitled to show anger in this way. The *śuddha-bhaktas* or *sad-gurus*, who have love for the *jīvas*, are entitled to do so. They can punish for they can do real good for others. We need their grace. Without the grace of Hari we cannot get the *sādhu*, and without the grace of the *sādhu* we cannot get Hari. If you are very keen to get the service of Krishna, Krishna will come to you in the form of the *sādhu*. When you have the sincere desire to serve Krishna you will get the knowledge to recognize who is a real *sādhu* and who is not. God is within you and He will help you to find the *sādhu*. He will give you faith and the capacity to understand. A sincere soul will never be deceived.

In many cultures, time is divided into four periods: the ages of gold, silver, bronze and iron. In the Vedas these are called *satya*, *tretā*, *dvāparā* and *kali*, respectively. Others may attribute different lengths of time to these ages, but the idea is the same: infinite time has been divided into four, recurring ages. As these ages pass we see a gradual deterioration of the human condition from happiness and innocence to sorrow and ignorance. It reaches its nadir in the present *kali-yuga*, the iron age. In this black age, persons will be mostly irreligious and therefore it is very difficult to find a bona fide guru. The Supreme Lord Śrī Krishna saw the plight of humanity in this black age, so He took the complexion and mode of worship of Rādhārāṇi and appeared as Śrī Chaitanya Mahāprabhu. Rādhā is Krishna's absolute counterpart; She is His best devotee and He has taken Her attitude to become Krishna Chaitanya.

Chaitanya Mahāprabhu said that the root cause of our affliction is forgetfulness of our relation with the Supreme Lord. We have to remember Him; if we can remember Him, there will be no afflictions. How we can do this? Through meditation? In this *kali-yuga* the method of meditation will not be successful because the enslaved *jīvas*' minds are restless. The mind is always jumping about like a monkey so how can we meditate? Nothing but worldly things will come to our mind. Simply by closing our eyes we are not meditating. We close our eyes and off we go to London. This is inevitable because the mind is like a storehouse of impressions that have entered it through the senses. When we try to meditate, these impressions come back up to the surface again.

We are attached to worldly things and this is the source of our bondage. In order to become free from this bondage, we should offer the objects of our attachment to the service of Krishna. This is the only way we can transcend our worldly attachments. The purpose is to concentrate on the transcendental object of worship, Lord Krishna.

In the *satya-yuga*, meditation was possible. The people of this age had purity, compassion, and respect for truthfulness. But in the *tretā-yuga*, these qualities diminished and the method of meditation on the Supreme Lord ceased to be possible. So the sages prescribed *yajña*, sacrifice. In the *dvāparā-yuga*, however, people could not utter the mantras correctly so the sages and scriptures prescribed worship of the deity form of the Lord. You have to engage all the senses to worship the deity. The goal is to develop concentration on the object of worship, and in order to do so you have to engage all your senses in the service of the deity. In the *kali-yuga*, however, we are so diseased that we cannot even perform proper *pūjā*. In this age, our physical and mental health is very fragile. We are all diseased and since a diseased person is prohibited from worship, how can we perform proper *pūjā*? So the Lord said, "You can perform *harināma*, you can chant the Holy Name. I shall appear in this world as *harināma* and give all power to *harināma*."

By chanting the Holy Name you can get the highest thing. In the *kali-yuga*, Truth means the Holy Name. The Holy Name is the Supreme Truth. Krishna appears in this *kali-yuga* as the Name. So take shelter of the Name. The Name and the Named are one. Chant the Holy Name in the company of a *śuddha-bhakta*.

The Holy Name is not a material sound. You will find the thing referred to by a material sound is different from the sound itself. The word "water" refers to the substance water. The word "water" is different from this substance. Thus we cannot quench our thirst by simply uttering the word "water." By way of contrast, Krishna and the name of Krishna are one and the same.

Chaitanya Mahāprabhu has written:

ceto-darpaṇa mārjanaṁ bhava-mahā-
dāvāgni-nirvāpanaṁ

śreyaḥ-kairava-candrikā-vitaraṇaṁ
vidyā-vadhū-jīvanam
anandāmbudhi-vardhanaṁ prati-padaṁ
pūrṇāmṛtāsvādanaṁ
sarvātma-snapanaṁ paraṁ vijayate
śrī kṛṣṇa-saṅkīrtanam

Utter Krishna's name from the core of your heart—Hare Krishna. You will get everything. Your mind will be sanctified. All difficulties will be removed by uttering His Name. This is the first attainment. Once all difficulties have been removed, you will no longer be confronted by the forest fire of material life. There is a forest fire throughout the whole world because everybody has a false ego and thinks he or she belongs to this world. But if we love Krishna, then we see that every living being is related to Krishna and we love them because of this relation. Parents need not be taught to love their children. They love them automatically because of their relation. So we have to take shelter of Śrī Krishna.

In Goloka Vṛndāvana, everyone is drowned in the *ānanda*. At every step they experience the sweetest ever-increasing ecstasy, because everybody's target is to satisfy Krishna. Their center is one. If you draw different circles with a single center, there will be no intersection. But if they have different centers, the circles will intersect, and there will be clashes. As long as there are different groups and different centers, we cannot stop fighting in this world. This material forest fire can be extinguished by *Harināma*, by chanting the *mahāmantra*:

hare kṛṣṇa hare kṛṣṇa, kṛṣṇa kṛṣṇa hare hare
hare rāma hare rāma, rāma rāma hare hare

We should chant the Holy Name without wanting anything other than the service of guru and Krishna. What is the meaning of *Śri-kṛṣṇa-saṅkīrtana*? *Saṅkīrtana* means to sing and chant about the transcendental glories, names, forms, attributes, and pastimes of Śrī Krishna entirely, exhaustively, and fully. We have to perform *saṅkīrtana* properly, avoiding the tenfold offenses.

Ten main offenses in the chanting of the Holy Name are listed in the *Padma Purāṇa*. The principal offense is to disgrace the *sadhus* and to think of the guru as an ordinary human being. How can Śrī Krishna tolerate it if we discredit or disparage those who are dear to Him? How can the Lord tolerate it if we commit offenses to their lotus feet? If we commit offenses to their lotus feet, than how can the Lord tolerate it? It is the greatest offense, and we should take every step to avoid making it.

We should always analyze ourselves and our own defects for this will help us to rectify ourselves. The greatest drawback of the conditioned souls, the enslaved *jīvas*, is that in themselves they only see good qualities while in others they only see defects. But we should not see the defects of the Vaiṣṇavas and devotees even if they have some. We should rather look to our own defects while taking care to observe the qualities of others. Then we can make progress. The tendency to find fault leads us to commit offenses to the Vaiṣṇavas. This is why Chaitanya Mahāprabhu has taught us the way to perform *Śri-kṛṣṇa-saṅkīrtana*: We should be more humble than a blade of grass, more tolerant than a tree, give respect to all others, and not demand any respect for ourselves. If we chant the *mahāmantra* with this attitude from the core of the heart, we will achieve our eternal welfare. Then we will get the knowledge that we are of Krishna and that we are His eternal servants.

hare kṛṣṇa hare kṛṣṇa, kṛṣṇa kṛṣṇa hare hare
hare rāma hare rāma, rāma rāma hare hare

We must cry to Rādhārānī and Krishna from the core of our heart. If we do, then Krishna will come to us immediately. He is within us, and He has given all power to His name. If we utter His name in consciousness of our relation to Him, we will be submerged in the ocean of *ānanda* and Krishna *prema*. After that, whenever we utter the Name we will experience infinite, complete ambrosia at every step. Hare Krishna.

PART THREE

Prayojana

The fulfillment of devotion

Prayojana

What is the ultimate goal of life (*prayojana*) for all living beings in this world? The ultimate goal is divine love for Śrī Krishna. We should speak on this subject throughout the year not just for half an hour. We should speak on this subject wherever we go.

Viśvanātha Cakravartī, a great Indian saint of Caitanya Mahāprabhu's school of thought, has given the substance of Caitanya Mahāprabhu's teachings in a Sanskrit verse:

ārādhyo bhagavān vrajeśa-tanayas
tad-dhāma vṛndāvanaṁ
ramyā kācid upāsanā vraja-vadhū-
vargeṇa yā kalpitā
śrīmad-bhāgavataṁ pramāṇam amalaṁ
premā pumartho mahān
śrī-chaitanya-mahāprabhor matam idaṁ
tatrādaro naḥ paraḥ

Who is the highest object of worship? Śrī Krishna is. Here Chaitanya Mahāprabhu is speaking about Vrajendra-nandana Krishna, the son of Nanda Mahārāja, the king of Vraja. Vraja means "where the cows graze." Nanda Mahārāja is the king (*indra*) of the cowherds (the *gopas* and *gopīs*). The son of Nanda Mahārāja, Nanda-nandana Śrī Krishna, is the highest object of worship. Nanda-nandana means the "son of Nanda." Vṛndāvana is the transcendental realm of Nanda-nandana Krishna, and He performs many kinds of pastimes there.

Now why has Chaitanya Mahāprabhu instructed us to worship Nanda-nandana Krishna? Chaitanya Mahāprabhu has not instructed us to worship demigods. He did not instruct us to worship *Paramātmā*, the object of worship of the yogīs. Nor has He instructed us to worship *Brahman* and merge in this formless aspect of the Absolute, the object of the *jñānīs*. He has not even taught us to worship the various forms of Krishna that have been displayed in numerous pastimes, such as Rāma, Narasiṁha, or Vāmana. Also, during His pastimes, Krishna, appears as Mathurādhīśa Krishna, Kurukṣetra Krishna, and Dvārakadhīśa Krishna. But Chaitanya Mahāprabhu has specifically stated that we should worship Nanda-nandana Śrī Krishna. Why?

The answer is that we can worship Nanda-nandana Krishna in the context of any possible relationship we desire. On the other hand, we cannot participate in all types of relationships with the Supreme Lord in His form of Nārāyaṇa. Nārāyaṇa displays a majestic form of God, so we can only have a relationship of friendship with Him from a distance. Persons fear going near to Nārāyaṇa because He is playing the role of a majestic king. His devotees may become His friends, but their intimacy is inhibited by fear. Moods like parental affection and conjugal love are absent. Thus those who wish to serve the Supreme Lord as a firm bosom friend, as their son or in a mood of conjugal love, cannot acquire this sort of relationship with the Lord in His Nārāyaṇa form. Therefore, Nārāyaṇa cannot be the common center for all devotees.

In Krishna, the cowherdboy of Vṛndāvana, however, all sorts of intimate relationships are possible and, of all these various forms of worship, the amorous worship of the *gopīs* for Krishna is the highest. The *gopīs* have engaged all their senses to the fullest extent for the service of Śrī Krishna, and amongst the *gopīs*, Śrī Rādhā, the absolute counterpart of Śrī Krishna, is the best. She is the personification of His internal potency of ecstatic love and Her devotion to Krishna is beyond comparison.

In Krishna we find twelve *rasas*. *Rasa* is the mellow of the relationship, the taste or bliss one experiences in a particular relationship with Krishna. There are five primary *rasas* (*mukhya-rasas*), namely *śānta* (neutrality), *dāsya* (servitude), *sakhya* (friendship), *vātsalya* (parenthood) and *mādhurya* (consorthood). In addition there are seven secondary or *gauṇa-rasas*, namely *hāsya* (laughter), *adbhuta* (astonishment), *vīra* (heroism), *karuṇa* (compassion), *raudra* (anger), *bhayānaka* (fear), and *bībhatsa* (disgust). All these *rasas* are described in *Śrīmad Bhāgavatam*. There, it is related how the evil king Kaṁsa tried to kill Krishna. Kaṁsa thought, "I will built a great stadium. I shall invite all the inhabitants of Mathurā and Vraja to come there to participate. There will be a wrestling match. The wrestlers will fight with Krishna and His brother Balarāma and kill them." So Kaṁsa made arrangements and many visitors came to watch the wrestling in the great stadium. When Krishna and His elder brother Balarāma made Their entrance into the wrestling arena, all the spectators saw Krishna in different ways.

mallānām aśanir nṛṇāṁ nara-varaḥ
strīṇāṁ smaro mūrtimān
gopānāṁ sva-jano satāṁ kṣiti-bhujāṁ
śāstā sva-pitroḥ śiśuḥ
mṛtyur bhoja-pater virāḍ aviduṣāṁ
tattvaṁ paraṁ yogināṁ
vṛṣṇīnāṁ para-devateti vidito
raṅgaṁ gataḥ sāgrajaḥ
(*Śrīmad Bhāgavatam* 10.43.17)

All the twelve *rasas* were thus manifested there. The first was *vīra-rasa*: the warrior *rasa*. The wrestlers saw Krishna in this way. The ordinary spectators saw Krishna as a wonderful human being: *adbhuta-rasa*. All the *gopīs* were there and they saw Krishna as their most beloved husband—*strīṇāṁ smaro mūrtimān*.

All the friends of Krishna saw Him as their friend—*gopānāṁ sva-jano*. A joking mood (*hāsya-rasa*) can also be found in relations between friends. For example, Krishna's *sakhā* (friend) Madhumaṅgala steals Krishna's sweets and creates a humorous atmosphere. The humorous *rasa* is a secondary or *gauṇa-rasa*, but the principal *rasa* is the *sakhya-rasa* or relation of frienship. In this *sakhya-rasa*, we see that the *hāsya-rasa* inspires feelings of love.

Those who were of an oppressive nature were afraid when they saw Krishna. They thought that their punisher had come. They were very much afraid, because they saw Krishna as angry and wrathful. This is *bhayānaka-rasa*. And all the parents saw their beloved child when they saw Krishna—*sva-pitoḥ śiśuḥ*. This is *vātsalya-rasa*. *Karuṇa-rasa* also plays a part in parental affection. *Karuṇa* means feelings of sympathy or pity. When they saw the sort of thing that was happening before them—a small child was opposing those formidable wrestlers—they felt pity. So this *karuṇa-rasa* is included in parental rasa.

Next, Kaṁsa thought death had come to him—*mṛtyur bhoja-pater*. He saw Krishna as something dreadful. Krishna is not dreadful, but that is how Kaṁsa saw Him. The ignorant saw Him as a mere man—*virāḍ aviduṣāṁ*. The yogis saw Krishna as the Supreme Truth in *śānta-rasa* while the Yādavas saw Krishna in *dāsya-rasa*, the mood of service. So, we can find all the five principle *rasas* and seven secondary *rasas* in Krishna alone. We can experience all kinds of *rasas* by serving Krishna, but we cannot obtain the same result by serving any other form of the Lord.

Kavirāja Gosvāmī has written in *Chaitanya Caritāmṛta* that fifty kinds of divine qualities can be found in the *jīvā* souls in minute quantity. Five more divine qualities can be found to a fuller extent in Śiva and Brahmā. Again, five more qualities are present in their full form in Nārāyaṇa or Viṣṇu. This makes a total of sixty divine characteristics or qualities in all. Now, there are four other qualities that you will not find anywhere else except in Krishna. These qualities are the incomparable sweetness of Krishna's *līlā* (*līlā-mādhurya*), the sweetness of His form (*rūpa-mādhurya*), the sweet sound of His flute (*veṇu-mādhurya*), and the sweetness of His love (*prema-mādhurya*). Krishna has many wonderful pastimes in which He assumes a sweet form. He does not appear in a very gigantic figure with all kinds of weapons. Thus, He does not fight with Pūtaṇā, the witch, but rather appearing as a baby He kills her by sucking her breast, exhibiting sweetness toward her. This is the wonder of Krishna's *līlā*. Also we find that even while keeping His own sweet form, Krishna lifts the mountain, Govardhana, with the small finger of His left hand. He does not assume a very great and strong figure to do this. As a small boy Krishna subdued Kāliya, a great serpent, when He jumped on Kāliya's thousands of heads. In no other form of God will you find such wonderful pastimes.

Krishna's associates are also very sweet. His *sakhās* climb on His shoulders to pluck fruit from the tops of the trees. They then taste the fruits to see whether they are good before giving them to Krishna. So much affection! So much intimacy! There is no majestic aspect in Vraja. There they think of Krishna as their own bosom friend. Krishna's parents love Him as their very own son. And Krishna's mother Yaśodā Devī even tries to discipline Him, thinking that otherwise His future will be bad... God's future will be bad!! And Nanda Mahārāja, with great affection, says to Krishna, "O Lālā, bring my slippers." What is this? He is ordering Bhagavān to bring him his slippers!! So, Krishna runs to fetch the slippers and puts them on His head. Observing this, Nanda Mahārāja thinks that his son will grow up to be very good. Krishna and Nanda Mahārāja run toward each other and they embrace.

Be that as it may, we cannot compare the *gopīs'* love for Krishna to anything else. It is incomparable. And the sound of Krishna's flute! When the *gopīs* hear the sound of the flute they run toward Krishna, leaving behind all other duties and even their own babies. All the mountains melt upon hearing the *vaṁśī-dhvani*: the sound of

Krishna's flute. By hearing this sound the river Yamunā begins to flow in the opposite direction. All is so beautiful that even Krishna is attracted by His own beauty and love. There is no one greater than or equal to Him.

Because of Krishna's sweetness Brahmā, who has been designated the task of creation by the Supreme Lord, could not recognize Him as the Supreme Lord. Brahmā did not believe it when he heard that Krishna, the cowherd boy from Vraja, was God. He thought, "How can He be *Svayaṁ-Bhagavān*? He is the son of Nanda Mahārāja, a milkman and one of my created beings. He cannot be Bhagavān. A cowherd boy has no opulences—nothing! Bhagavān is the possessor of all opulences, but this Krishna is walking in the jungle with cowherd boys and has no valuable possessions. He wears a garland of forest flowers and has a peacock feather in His hair. How can anyone say that He is Bhagavān? A peasant cannot be Bhagavān."

Now, at that time there was a demon named Aghāsura who wanted to kill Krishna and the cowherd boys. Aghāsura took the form of a giant snake and opened his mouth wide so that from a distance the cowherd boys thought they were seeing a nice cave. They also saw a road leading to the cave, which was actually the tongue of the snake-demon. So thinking Aghāsura's mouth to be a cave, the cowherd boys walked into it and the demon immediately swallowed them. When Krishna saw what had happened, He decided to save His friends. He followed them into the demon's mouth and started to expand Himself. His body became bigger and bigger and by so doing blocked the snake's throat. The snake could not breath anymore and soon died of suffocation. When he saw that Krishna had killed the demon Aghāsura, Brahmā began to wonder, "How could this mere cowherd boy kill such a giant demon?" He then decided to find out whether Krishna was Bhagavān or not.

In the meantime, Krishna, being very fond of picnics, came to the bank of a lake with His friends. The cowherd boys had brought some food for Krishna and had hung it in the trees at the picnic spot earlier so that no one could take it. When they came to that spot, they took their lunch bags down from the trees and began to feed Krishna—but only after testing the food by tasting it first. If it was good they would say: "Hey Krishna! Kanhaiyā! This tastes good, try some!" Then they would give it to Krishna.

Brahmā came there at that moment and when he saw Krishna taking the remnants of all of the cowherd boys, he again thought, "This cannot be Bhagavān—He is nothing more than a peasant." Brahmā also saw a mixture of curd and rice in Krishna's left hand. The Vedic scriptures enjoin that one should take food from the right hand, not the left. So Brahmā thought, "He does not know right from left, He cannot be Bhagavān. He is nothing but an ignorant rustic." He also saw that Krishna kept a flute tucked inside His waistband and a horn under His armpit. All the cowherd boys were addressing Him in a familiar manner instead of using words of respect. Brahmā thought, "Bhagavān should be respected from a distance with prostrated obeisances. One should pay respects to Him with the appropriate formal speech. How could Bhagavān tolerate this behavior?"

At one point, the cowherd boys said to Krishna, "We have to go and get the calves, otherwise it will be late when we get back home." But Krishna replied, "No, you stay here and rest, I will get the calves." Now, when Krishna went looking for the calves, He could not find them because Brahmā had stolen them and had hidden them in a cave. Krishna became sad and asked everyone He saw, "Our calves are lost, have you seen them? How can I go back home without them?"

By the time Krishna had returned to the picnic spot, Brahmā had also stolen all the cowherd boys and taken them to the same cave in Mount Sumeru where he had earlier hidden the calves. Now that He had lost all the calves and the cowherd boys, Krishna sat down and wept. Brahmā observed this and smiled. He thought with great satisfaction, "Bhagavān knows everything. If Krishna were the Supreme Lord, He could have taken back the calves forcibly. But He does not know where the calves and boys are and He is incapable of recovering them. So I was right, He is just an ordinary cowherd boy." And so he left.

After Brahmā had gone, Krishna also smiled and expanded Himself into as many calves and cowherd boys as Brahmā had stolen. Thus when He returned home, the cows were not even aware that they had lost their calves, and the *gopas* and *gopīs* were equally unaware that they had lost their children. Everything is possible for Krishna. To fulfill the desires of the *gopas* and *gopīs* who would have liked to have Him as their son, Krishna came to them as their sons. The *gopas* and *gopīs* had always thought that Nanda and Yaśodā were so lucky to have Krishna as their son. Now that He came to them as their own sons, they could not recognize Him, but as soon as they touched them, they experienced an overwhelming sense of love that can only be obtained from Krishna. They drowned in the ocean of *ānanda*.

The cows of Vṛndāvana were not ordinary cows. They had all been sages in their previous lives. Cows normally have affection for their own young calves, but now that Krishna had taken the form of their calves, they tore the ropes that bound them and went rushing toward them. They were even running through thorns and getting cut and were bleeding all over, such was the extent of their love. Due to their yearning for Krishna, Krishna Himself had come as their calves to suckle their breasts. Krishna came for an entire year for that reason alone—to satisfy them and fulfill their desires.

After one year, Brahmā came back. He saw the same calves and cowherd boys that had been there before. He thought, "Impossible! It can't be. I imprisoned them all in the mountain cave. I cannot understand this." Thinking in this way, he went back to the cave in Mount Sumeru and saw that the same calves and same cowherd boys were still sleeping there. Once again he returned to Vṛndāvana and saw that the cows and cowherd boys were there as well. Brahmā could then understand the situation and he thought, " All creatures are deluded by my illusions, but now I myself have been deluded by my Master." He then took absolute shelter of Krishna and prayed for forgiveness. Once he had taken shelter, Krishna was gracious and came and showed Brahmā His majestic four-handed Vāsudeva form in each of the cowherd boys and in each of the calves. Brahmā then said:

naumīḍya te 'bhra-vapuṣe taḍid-ambarāya
guñjāvataṁsa-paripiccha-lasan-mukhāya
vanya-sraje kavala-vetra-viṣāṇa-veṇu-
lakṣma-śriye mṛdu-pade paśupāṅgajāya
(*Śrīmad Bhāgavatm* 10.14.1)

"You are the highest object of worship. I know this to be true You are the cause of all causes, the source of all *avatāras*. You are the possessor of all *rasas*. Your body is the color of the rain-bearing clouds. Your garment is brilliant like lightning, and the beauty of Your face is enhanced by Your guñjā earrings and the peacock feather in your hair. Wearing garlands of various forest flowers and leaves, and equipped with a herding stick, a buffalo horn and a flute, You stand beautifully with a morsel of food in Your hand."

Thus Brahmā recognized the supremacy of the sweetest of lords, Śrī Krishna. Nowhere in the entire creation is there any comparison.

In Krishna *līlā* we find that one day, there were no servants in Nanda Mahārāja's house. So mother Yaśodā went herself to churn butter from the milk. While she was churning the milk, the young child Krishna came to her. Krishna had just learned how to walk and was playing the pastime of being hungry. He said, "O mother, stop churning, I am hungry. Give me milk!" To this Yaśodā replied, "There are no servants here and so I am busy. Don't disturb me."

After hearing this, Krishna, with His beautiful small hand, grabbed hold of the churning stick. Yaśodā was charmed and put the child on her lap to breastfeed Him, but at that very instant, the milk on the stove started to boil over. So, Yaśodā said to Gopāla, "Get down, the milk is boiling." But Krishna's appetite had not been appeased and He did not want to get down. He said, "Give me more milk." Yaśodā thrust Krishna down and ran to the stove. Krishna became very angry because of this and wanted to break the pot containing the yogurt. Though He was still afraid of His mother, He silently struck the pot with a small stone until it broke and all the curd spilled onto the floor. Then, seeing other pots hanging from the ceiling, He climbed onto the mortar and broke them all.

Sometimes the other *gopīs* complained to Yaśodā and Nanda Mahārāja. They complained that Krishna was very naughty and would come to their houses at night. They said, "We light lamps to keep the thieves away, but your boy blows them out. Then He steals our butter." Nanda would ask Krishna, "Kanhaiyā, did you do this?" "No father, I did not. They are telling lies." Krishna put on a very innocent face, like a *sādhu* or a saint. When His parents saw this innocent expression, they thought it impossible that He could have done such a thing. Nanda Mahārāja would answer the *gopīs*' charges, "I have thousands of cows. I am the king of Vraja. Why should my son go to another house to steal butter?" The reason was that Krishna sometimes wanted to go to other people's houses to give them a chance to serve Him. Normally His parents would not allow Him to go anywhere else to eat. They love Krishna too much themselves. That is why He sometimes acts like a thief, to give all His devotees a chance to serve Him, to fulfill their desires. So, outwardly, it seemed as though Krishna was destroying everything and spoiling the yogurt by eating it and feeding it to the monkeys. In fact, the yogurt had been prepared from the milk of cows who desired that it be used in His service. So actually Krishna was giving everybody a chance to serve Him in this way.

When Yaśodā returned from the stove she saw what mischief Krishna had wrought. He had destroyed all the pots and was feeding the monkeys. As a result, she wanted to punish Him. She thought, "If I do not teach Him a lesson, His character will be spoiled." So, Yaśodā decided to cane the Supreme Lord Bhagavān to correct His character. She approached Krishna silently, hoping to catch Him by surprise. But just when she was about to catch Him, Krishna jumped up and ran away. Soon Yaśodā was chasing Krishna all over the courtyard, but she quickly became tired and started to move more slowly. Though nobody is able to catch Krishna, He Himself slowed down and allowed her to catch Him because of her pure affection for Him.

Yaśodā said, "What have you done? I shall cane you!" Krishna was afraid of the cane in His mother's hand

and started to cry. Even the god of death fears Krishna, the Supreme Lord, but He is afraid when He sees a cane in the hand of His mother. How is it possible? This is Vraja *prema*. The Vrajavasis do not see Krishna as God. They only love Him with all their hearts.

Then Yaśodā felt pity for Krishna and decided instead to fasten Him with some rope so He could do no more mischief. She tried to tie the rope around His belly, but it was two inches too short. Again and again she brought more rope, but it was always too short. So though we see on the one hand that Krishna was limited like a small boy, in fact He is unlimited even in His apparent limitation.

Why was the rope always two inches short? What is the significance of this? One inch represents the grace of Krishna, the other, the sincere service with which we can attract His grace. Yaśodā never stops in her service of Krishna, and that is why in the end Krishna allowed her to bind Him with the ropes of her love. We must also make the same kind of sincere effort to serve Guru and Vaiṣṇava; then we will be able to attract their grace.

Śrīla Rūpa Gosvāmī has written this song:

bandhu saṅge jadi taba raṅga parihas thāke abhilāṣ
tabe mor kathā rākha jeyo nāka jeyo nāka

vṛndāvane keśītīrtha ghāter sakāś
nayane baṅkima-dṛṣṭi mukhe manda-hās

"If you still desire to amuse yourself with your friends, you should not go to Vṛndāvana. And if you go to Vṛndāvana, you should especially not go to Keśi Ghat. There is a danger lurking there. What is that danger? It is Śrī Hari, Krishna Himself, who has taken the form of Govinda, *Govinda vigraha dhari*. The danger is that if you go there and see Him, if you have a vision of Govinda, you will not be able to return to the customary amusements of your ordinary household life."

The look of His eyes, His crooked glance is very dangerous—*nayane baṅkima-dṛṣṭi mukhe manda-hās*. He is not standing straight, but in *tri-bhaṅga*, with three curves. If this Krishna enters you, He will not come out. If Narāyāṇa enters, He may come out. Narāyāṇa is straight. But Krishna is curved like a hook and that is dangerous.

His color is like that of a rain cloud—*varṇa samujjvala śyāma*. You will find that in the springtime the leaves of the trees are so fresh. Similarly, Krishna is not old, but a young adolescent. The lips of His mouth are very dangerous and if you see the peacock feather on His head, you will not be able to come back to your household life. So, if you want to have fun with your friends, you should not go to Vṛndāvana, and you should not look at Krishna.

Unfortunately, we go to Vṛndāvana and still come

back. We do not have such devotion. If anybody truly had the greed for Govinda, he could not return to his mundane life. His worldly relations would be destroyed. Greed for devotion is developed by associating with the pure devotees of the Lord. By their grace it becomes possible for us to attain Krishna *prema*, divine love of God, the ultimate goal of life.

Pronunciation Guide

The system of transliteration used in this book conforms to a system that scholars have accepted to indicate the pronunciation of each sound in the Sanskrit language.

The short vowel a is pronounced like the **u** in b**u**t, long **ā** like the **a** in f**a**r. The short i is pronounced as in p**i**n, the long **ī** as in p**i**que, the short **u** as in p**u**ll, and the long **ū** as in r**u**le.

The vowel **ṛ** is pronounced like the **ri** in **ri**m, **e** like the **ey** in th**ey**, **o** like the **o** in g**o**, **ai** like the **ai** in **ai**sle, and **au** like the **ow** in h**ow**.

The *anusvāra* (**ṁ**) is pronounced like the **n** in the French word bo**n**, and *visarga* (**ḥ**) is pronounced as a final **h** sound. At the end of a couplet **aḥ** is pronounced as **aha**, and **iḥ** is pronounced as **ihi**.

The guttural consonants **-k**, **kh**, **g**, **gh**, and **ṇ-** are pronounced from the throat in much the same manner as in English. **K** is pronounced as in **k**ite, **kh** as in Ec**kh**art, **g** as in **g**ive, **gh** as in di**g h**ard, **ṅ** as in si**ng**.

The palatal consonants **-c**, **ch** , **j**, **jh** and **ñ-** are pronounced with the tongue touching the firm ridge behind the teeth. **C** is pronounced as in **ch**air, **ch** as in staun**ch-h**eart, **j** as in **j**oy, **jh** as in hed**geh**og, and **ñ** as in ca**n**yon.

The cerebral consonants **-ṭ, ṭh, ḍ, ḍh, ṇ-** are pronounced with the tip of the tongue turned up and drawn back against the dome of the palate. **Ṭ** is pronounced as in **t**ub, **ṭh** as in ligh**t-h**eart, **ḍ** as in **d**ove, **ḍh** as in re**d-h**ot, and **ṇ** as in **n**ut.

The dental consonants **-t, th, d, dh,** and **n-** are pronounced in the same manner as the cerebrals, but with the forepart of the tongue against the teeth.

The labial consonants **-p, ph, b, bh,** and **m-** are pronounced with the lips. **P** is pronounced as in **p**ine, **ph** as in u**ph**ill, **b** as in **b**ird, **bh** as in ru**b-h**ard, and **m** as in **m**other.

The semivowels **-y, r, l,** and **v-** are pronounced as in **y**es, **r**un, **l**ight, and **v**ine respectively.

The sibilants **-ś, ṣ,** and **s-** are pronounced, respectively, as in the German word **s**prechen and the English words **sh**ine and sun. The letter **h** is pronounced.

Abhidheya: the means of attaining the ultimate goal of life (see also *sādhana*).

Ahaṅkāra: false ego; the most subtle material layer that covers the spirit soul (*jīva*).

Ānanda: ecstatic bliss.

Aparā śakti: material potency of the Lord (see also *māyā-śakti*).

Ātmā: soul; either refers to the individual soul (*jīvātmā*) or the Supersoul (*paramātmā*).

Avatāra: divine descent; the Supreme Lord appearing in this world in His own transcendental form (without accepting a physical body), to carry out a specific task, like re-establishing the principles of religion or killing the demoniac.

Avatāri: the original form from which all *avatāras* originate; Supreme Lord Śrī Krishna.

Bhagavān: God or Krishna, the possessor of six opulences–all majesty, all prowess, all fame, all beauty, all wisdom and all detachment.

Bhakta: devotee.

Bhakti: devotion to God.

Brahmā: the creator of the Universe, designated to this task by Lord Krishna.

Brahman: the all-pervading effulgence coming from the transcendental body of Lord Krishna; the impersonal aspect of Godhead.

Buddhi: intelligence.

Chaitanya Mahāprabhu: The divine descent (*avatāra*) of Lord Krishna, appearing 500 years ago to inaugurate the congregational chanting of the Holy Names for attaining love of God, the religion for *kali-yuga.*

Cit: pure consciousness.

Darśana: seeing the divine.

Dāsya-rasa: mellow of servitude in relation to Śrī Krishna.

Gauṇa-rasa: the seven secondary rasas, namely: *hāsya-*, *adbhuta-*, *vīra-*, *karuṇa-*, *raudra-*, *bhayānaka-* and *vī-bhatsa-rasa.* These correspond respectively to laughter, astonishment, heroism, compassion, anger, fear, and disgust.

Gopa: cowherd boy; eternal associates of Krishna in Vṛndāvana, who serve Him in the mood of bosom-friends. See also *sakhā.*

Gopī: cowherd girl; eternal associates of Krishna in Vṛndāvana, headed by Śrīmatī Rādhārāni, who serve Him in the mood of amorous love. See also *sakhī.*

Guṇa: (1) quality or mode of material nature, three in number: *sattva-*, *rajo-* and *tamo-guṇa.* (2) Krishna's transcendental qualities.

Guru: one who is 'heavy' with transcendental knowledge; spiritual preceptor.

Hari: another name for God or Krishna.
Harināma: indicates the glorification and singing of the Names of Krishna.
Jīva: (or *jīvātma*) individual atomic soul.
Jīva-śakti: the marginal potency of the Lord, from where unlimited *jīvas* manifest.
Jñāna: knowledge aimed at impersonal *brahman*-realization, resulting in liberation.
Jñāni: practitioner of *jñāna*.
Kali-yuga: the fourth and most degraded of the cosmic ages. According to the Vedas this age started 5000 years ago and will last another 427,000 years.
Kāma: lust.
Karma: (1) materially motivated action which yields an equal and opposite reaction (fate). (2) reward-seeking activity.
Karmi: practitioner of *karma*.
Krishna: the original bhagavān, the Supreme Lord and avatāri, Who performs His eternal *līlā* as a cowherd-boy in Goloka Vṛndāvana (see also *Vṛndāvana*).
Līlā: the transcendental sportive pastimes of Lord Krishna.
Mādhurya-rasa: mellow of consorthood in relation to Śrī Krishna.
Manas: the mind.
Māyā: illusion.
Māyā-śakti: illusory potency of the Lord. (see also

aparā śakti).

Nāma-saṅkīrtana: congregational chanting of the Holy Names of the Lord; best method for *Kali-yuga* to attain love of God, the ultimate goal of life.

Mukhya-rasa: the five primary *rasas*, namely: *śānta-*, *dāsya-*, *sakhya-*, *vātsalya-*, and *mādhurya-rasa.*

Parā śakti: spiritual potency of the Lord (see also svarūpa-śakti).

Paramātmā: the Supersoul, the form of Krishna residing in the heart of every living being.

Prasāda: sanctified remnants of the articles offered to the Lord; usually refers to offered food.

Prayojana: the ultimate goal of life, *Krishna-prema.*

Prema: Divine love of God, the ultimate goal of life.

Pūjā: worship of the deity of the Lord with various items.

Rādhā: (also called Rādhārāṇī) the Absolute feminine counterpart of Lord Krishna; the most beloved of Krishna; the personification of Krishna's internal potency.

Rāga: spontaneous attraction.

Rāgānugā bhakti: *bhakti* that is awakened in the heart out of a spontaneous desire to serve the Lord affectionately in the wake of the Eternal Associates of Lord Krishna, known as *Rāgātmikās*.

Rāgātmikā bhakti: the loving devotion of the eternal associates of Lord Krishna for His divine pleasure alone, accompanied with complete self-effacement on the part of the eternal associates.

Raja-guṇa: the material mode of passion.

Rasa: 'taste' or 'juice', referring to the transcendental mellows that are experienced in relation to the Supreme Lord Śrī Krishna.

Sādhanā: spiritual practice.

Sādhu: saint; pure devotee.

Sakhā: transcendental boyfriend of Krishna.

Sakhī: transcendental girlfriend of Krishna.

Sakhya-rasa: mellow of friendship in relation to Śrī Krishna.

Śakti: potency.

Sambandha: relationship.

Saṅkīrtana: congregational glorification of the Lord.

Śānta-rasa: mellow of neutrality in relation to Śrī Krishna.

Śaraṇāgati: full surrender to Krishna or His representative, the spiritual master or *śuddha-bhakta*.

Sat: eternal.

Sattva-guṇa: the material mode of goodness.

Śiva: God of destruction.

Śraddhā: faith in the Lord which manifests in the association of *sādhus* as a result of previous pious deeds (*sukṛti*).

Śuddha: pure.

Śuddha-bhakta: pure devotee.
Śuddhā bhakti: pure devotion.
Sukṛti: pious activity which produces faith in the Lord and the process of *bhakti.*
Svarūpa-śakti: internal potency of the Lord (see also *parā śakti*).
Tamo-guṇa: the material mode of ignorance.
Upādhi: material designation.
Vaidhī-bhakti: regulated devotion, which follows the guidelines of the scriptures.
Vaiṣṇava: devotee of Viṣṇu or Krishna.
Vātsalya-rasa: mellow of parenthood in relation to Śrī Krishna.
Viṣṇu: the primary expansion of Krishna, who is in control of the material creation.
Vedas: the revealed scriptures of India.
Vraja: see *Vṛndāvana.*
Vrajavāsis: inhabitants of Vraja.
Vṛndāvana: "Forest of Vṛnda-trees", Transcendental abode of Lord Kṛṣṇa. The transcendental Vṛndāvana situated in the spiritual realm is called Goloka Vṛndāvana, whereas the earthly Vṛndāvana indicates the place where Krishna performed His manifest *līlā* 5000 years ago, as the tradition holds. This earthly Vṛndāvana is situated 120 kilometers south of the present city of New Delhi.
Yoga: (1) any spiritual discipline meant to link or

unite oneself with the Supreme; (2) practice of meditation.

Yogi: a person who practices self-control and meditative practices in order to attain salvation from material life.

Yuga: an age of the cosmic time cycle into which infinite time has been divided according to the *Vedas*. The four *yugas* are *Satya*, *Tretā*, *Dvāparā*, and *Kali*.

UPADEŚĀVALI

Śrīla Prabhupāda
Bhaktisiddhānta Sarasvati Ṭhākura

1. "*Paraṁ vijayate śrī kṛṣṇa saṇkīrtanam* - supreme victory to the congregational chanting of Krishna's names"- this is Śrī Gauḍīya Maṭha's sole object of worship.

2. Śrī Krishna, who is the *viṣaya-vigraha* or the object of the devotees *prema*, is the sole enjoyer and all others are to be enjoyed by Him.

3. Those who don't perform *hari-bhajana* are ignorant and murderers of their own souls.

4. The acceptance of *Śrī Harināma* and direct realization of Bhagavān are one and the same.

5. Those who equate the demigods with Viṣṇu are unable to serve Bhagavān.

6. Establishing a printing press to print devotional books and preaching by organizing *nāma-hāṭṭa* programs constitutes genuine service to Śrī Māyāpura.

7. We are not doers of good or bad deeds, nor are

we scholars or illiterate. Carrying the shoes of Hari's pure devotees as our duty, we are initiates into the mantra "*kīrtanayah sada hari*".

8. Preaching without proper conduct falls within the category of *karma*, mundane activity. Without criticizing the nature of others, one should correct one's self - this is my personal instruction.

9. Serving the Vrajavāsīs who felt great separation from Krishna when He left Vraja to reside in Mathurā is our supreme constitutional occupation.

10. If we desire to follow an auspicious course in life, then we should disregard the theories of even countless people and hear instructions from a transcendental source.

11. Life as an animal, bird, insect or any other of the countless thousands of species is acceptable, but taking shelter of deceit is thoroughly improper. Only an honest person possesses real auspiciousness.

12. Simple-heartedness is synonymous with Vaiṣṇavism. Servants of a *paramahaṁsa* Vaiṣṇava should be simple-hearted, a quality which makes them the topmost *brāhmaṇas*.

13. Helping to draw conditioned souls away from their perverted attachment to the material energy is the greatest compassion. If even one soul is rescued from *Mahāmāyā*'s fortress, that compassionate act is infinitely more benevolent than the construction of unlimited hospitals.

14. We have not come to this world to be construction workers; we are the bearers of Śrī Chaitanya's instructions.

15. We will not remain in this world for long, and by profusely performing *Hari-kīrtana*, upon relinquishing this material body we will experience the ultimate reward of embodied life.

16. The foot-dust of Śrī Rūpa Gosvāmī, the fulfiller of Śrī Chaitanyadeva's inner desires, is the desired object of our soul.

17. If I were to desist from lecturing about the Absolute Truth due to being fearful that some listeners may be displeased, I would be deviating from the path of Vedic truth and accepting the path of untruth. I would become one who is inimical to the Vedas, an atheist, and would no longer possess faith in Bhagavān, the very embodiment of truth.

18. Krishna's *darśana* can only be attained through the medium of the ear as one hears *Hari-kathā* from pure Vaiṣṇavas; there is no other way.

19. Wherever *Hari-kathā* is being spoken is a holy place.

20. Proper *śravaṇa*, hearing, is accomplished through the medium of *kīrtana*, and this will give one the good opportunity to practice *smaraṇa*, remembrance. Then the internal experience of rendering direct service to the *aṣṭa-kālīya-līlā*, Śrī Rādhā-Krishna's pastimes in each of the eight parts of the day, becomes possible.

21. We should understand that the loud calling out of Śrī Krishna's names is *bhakti*.

22. Bhagavān will not accept anything which is offered by a person who doesn't chant *Harināma* one hundred thousand times daily.

23. By sincerely endeavoring to chant *Harināma* without offenses and remaining fixed in chanting constantly, one's offenses will fade and pure *Harināma* will arise on one's tongue.

24. If mundane thoughts arise while taking *Harināma*, one should not become discouraged. A secondary consequence of taking *Harināma* is that these useless mundane thoughts will gradually dissipate; therefore one should not worry about this. By devoting one's mind, body and words to serving *Śrī Nāma* and continuing to chant with great persistence, *Śrī Nāma* Prabhu will grant one *darśana* of His supremely auspicious transcendental form. And by continuing to chant until one's *anarthas* are fully eradicated, realization of His form, qualities and pastimes will automatically arise by the power of *Śrī Nāma*.